To:-Dear Mike
Thank you so much for
all you've done for
the Claude 8
Here's loping n
togetha
Claudette P.J.
Dec 5, 2015

Children in the Line of Fire

THE IMPACT OF VIOLENCE AND TRAUMA ON FAMILIES IN JAMAICA AND TRINIDAD AND TOBAGO

Claudette Crawford-Brown

ARAWAK
publications
KINGSTON · JAMAICA

This book is dedicated to my parents:
To my mother Lillith Pearl Crawford, who taught me to "Never Give Up"
and
To my father Phillip Claudis Jackson Crawford, who will never see the
final script, but who speaks through this publication to his legacy

A r a w a k publications
17 Kensington Crescent, Unit 5
Kingston 5, Jamaica W.I.
www.arawakpublications.com

© 2010 by Claudette Crawford-Brown
    All rights reserved. Published 2010
    ISBN 978 976 95304 5 4

15 14 13 12 11 10   5 4 3 2 1

A RECORD OF CIP DATA IS AVAILABLE FROM
THE NATIONAL LIBRARY OF JAMAICA

Credits:
Cover art by Omar Brown Jr.

Set in 10.5/13pt Book Antiqua with Bernard MT Condensed
Printed in the United States of America

CONTENTS

APPENDIXES

Foreword

Retired Senior Lecturer,
Department of Sociology, Psychology & Social Work
University of the West Indies (Mona)

This is an important book for Jamaica and the Caribbean region. First, it locates the needs of children precisely where they should be most carefully considered: as the future adult populations of our societies and as the future of our national development. Dr. Crawford-Brown's book is an outcry about the conditions under which many children live, and the stresses which they undergo in our violent society. Our development prospects are threatened by the ways in which our children are growing up, and this is a concern not only to be noted by social welfare agencies, but by hard-headed economists at the International Monetary Fund and the World Bank.

Dr. Crawford-Brown points out the multiple economic and political vulnerabilities of our small postcolonial societies in the global environment, including widespread involvement in global criminal networks, and shows the ways in which these vulnerabilities play their ways out in the lives of our children. Also, living in a geographically vulnerable area of hurricanes, earthquakes, and volcanoes, she shows most poignantly how children interlink nature's violence with interpersonal and manmade violence. One child associates hurricanes with "looting and shooting". Another child is afraid of trees because "trees shoot at people". (Dr. Crawford-Brown later discovers that a gunman in the child's neighbourhood hides in trees to shoot at people, and this has generated the child's fear of all trees.)

What strikes the reader forcibly is how much Dr. Crawford-Brown herself needed to write this book. Her experiences of more than a decade are expressed through many illustrations. Some .are presented as statistics, some as case studies, some as a single child's drawing. She is showing us the crises of children in our society. What is of great concern, as she points out, is that these may be only the tip of the iceberg!

Dr. Crawford-Brown's work is also very prescient in having identified, years ago, some of the most pressing problems of today such as the children of migrants, children of incarcerated drug couriers, street children, and the sexual abuse of children with disabilities.

What can one concerned individual do? For more than fifteen years, Dr. Crawford-Brown has taught social work students at the University of the West Indies, Mona, using innovative practice methods including a Violence Prevention Clinic for Children and Families. She also has produced a wealth of counselling materials which, with the support of the United Nations Children's Fund (UNICEF), are being made available through the Ministry of Education to School Guidance Counsellors and other counselling professionals.

In this current publication, Dr. Crawford-Brown presents her deeply thought-out prescriptions and solutions. These are path-breaking, culturally relevant tools; she calls them, "interventions that work". She also gives broad policy recommendations, including a focus on our family and child-rearing behaviours. She calls for in-depth sociological analysis as a precursor for developing violence prevention programmes based on family and community. "We have to garner the resources of a nation to fight the scourge of violence affecting our children."

Dr. Crawford-Brown is to be congratulated on her outstanding effort to put the needs of our children before our eyes. The greatest joy of a teacher is to see her students excel, and I am honoured that Dr. Crawford-Brown lists me among her intellectual influences.

August 2010

PREFACE and OVERVIEW

The title "Children in the Line of Fire" emerged from a series of annual lectures given by the writer entitled "Violence and the Jamaican Child" prepared for an undergraduate course on Caribbean Social Problems at the University of the West Indies, Mona Campus, between 2002 and 2005. The title underlines the fact that children in Jamaica are not just caught up in the literal cross hairs of guns and other forms of violence, but are figuratively in the line of 'fire' from all of the major systems that make up the fabric of the society, namely from the macro (societal) perspective, the mezzo (community) perspective, as well as the micro (individual and family) perspective.

The book argues that children, who are often described as 'soft targets' in the ongoing crossfire involving various warring factions and systems, are some of the most serious casualties of the ongoing violence, and opines that, as a developing country aspiring to move into the twenty-first century, the entire Jamaican society and, by extension, Caribbean society, must be made to understand its role (in the short-term) in the protection of our children. At the same time, it suggests that in the medium and long term there must be a concerted and committed effort to understand the nature of the violence against children in all its dimensions so that its effects on children can be reduced and eventually eliminated in order to protect and safeguard our society's future. (For the case studies mentioned in the book, all names have been changed to protect the individuals, and place names are referred to as regions only.)

This book sets out in a detailed and systematic yet non-sensational manner the effects of violence and trauma in all its forms on children, adolescents and their families. It also sets out a blueprint for what the different sectors of the society must do in order to stem the scourge of violence sweeping across the islands of the Caribbean, consuming the most vulnerable sectors of our societies and the region's future, our children.

The arguments put forward in the book suggest that Jamaican society and by extension the Caribbean has been inattentive to the impact of violence and other social problems on the mental health of its children. If one assumes that an important criterion for measuring a country's development is its ability to protect its most vulnerable, the author opines that the country and the region are in danger of being in a state of persistent underdevelopment – a condition which the region can avoid with sound prevention and intervention policies. A nation that cannot protect its children is a nation that is in trouble, and one that can never truly be said to have developed, regardless of the economic indicators that may say otherwise. The purpose of this book therefore is not just to examine why there is so much violence against children but also to examine the factors that create obstacles to the children's protection.

The uniqueness of this book stems from the fact that it provides the reader with basic, easily readable information. This information ranges from the anatomy of violence – that is, the types of violence affecting children and families, the number of children and families affected – to the causes of the violence, how it develops, and how children become violent adults. Other issues discussed include the motives behind the violent acts and the issues surrounding the violence that make the Jamaican situation unique. The book also addresses the most frequently asked questions about violence affecting children, such as what are the underlying community and societal issues fuelling violence against children and their families.

About this book

The introductory chapter, "The Impact of Globalization on Caribbean Child Welfare", presents a statement of the effects of globalization on the Caribbean. It includes an overview of the global, regional and local issues impacting on crime and violence in the Caribbean region. This chapter also looks at the unique factors which make the region vulnerable to organized criminal activities and other forms of violence.

The first chapter, "Violence Affecting Children as Victims", represents a detailed description of the anatomy of violence against children who are victims of violence. It answers questions regarding the type and location of the violence, the age groups of the children impacted by this violence, the types of weapons used against these children and the motives for the various forms of violence affecting them.

The second chapter, "Children as Perpetrators – The Other Side of Violence", looks at those children who are perpetrators of violence or children who might be at risk of becoming perpetrators. This chapter analyses the policies that policymakers and practitioners need to be aware of in planning and working with this special cohort of children. This chapter is linked to the previous section which sets out how practitioners could best help different children depending on the specific issues presented.

The third chapter, "Parenting and Other Factors which Predispose Children to Violence", looks at the etiology of violent behaviour by examining the underlying causes of violent behaviour in children and adolescents. This discussion is grounded in empirical research conducted by the writer in the early 1990s. It goes on further to discuss the use of a predictive model of causation by analysing which specific variables are involved in the development of violent behaviour throughout the life cycle.

The fourth chapter, "In Their Own Words", uses illustrations drawn by the children themselves to describe the effect of violence in their homes, schools and communities. These illustrations were chosen from over 300 drawings done by children who were clients of the UWI Violence Prevention Programme, as well as children who attended summer classes conducted by the Programme between 2005 to 2006.

The fifth chapter, "The Effect of Violence on Children in Jamaica", looks at an analytical model developed by the writer to explain the 'Ah Nuh Nutten' (It is nothing) syndrome. The writer argues that children in Jamaica have developed a defense mechanism where they see violence as being of little consequence, in order to protect themselves psychologically. It is suggested that this phenomenon is widespread among children who would be expected to exhibit classic symptoms of trauma or depression, given the high levels of violence to which they are exposed. Many of these children however have developed 'scar tissue' as a maladaptive response to trauma as their way of coping with a situation over which they have little or no control. This chapter ends with the prototype of a Trauma Assessment Instrument for Caribbean Children (TAICC) which is accessible for use by readers for the purpose of testing validation and feedback to the author.

The sixth and final chapter, "Prescriptions and Solutions", looks in detail at the practical solutions that can be implemented in the society to deal with violence in the home, school and community.

This chapter makes reference to a pull-out section for practitioners in Appendix IX called "A Blueprint for Action", that can be used at PTA meetings and social agencies. This gives detailed guidelines to the user regarding what needs to be done with various violence related problems in the home, school and community.

Acknowledgments

The genesis of this publication was undoubtedly nurtured by the stimulating intellectual environment of the institution that is the University of the West Indies, which has acted as a protective crucible for the concepts, models and findings that have evolved from this publication.

I must express my appreciation to my peers and role models over the years, in particular, Hermione McKenzie and Barrington Chevannes of the Department of Sociology, Psychology and Social Work, who encouraged me in my academic pursuits over the years as I moved from being a student into the world of academia. These giants in sociological analysis, along with my peers, Clement Branche and Professors Anderson and Boxill stimulated in me very early on the desire for excellence in intellectual presentation and provided the encouragement necessary to produce and complete a project of this significance.

I must also acknowledge with a tremendous sense of gratitude the Principal's Research Fellowship Programme, which afforded me the time and resources to put this publication together. The programme released me from my normal teaching schedule and allowed me to work full time on this publication, which involved travel across three countries in pursuit of relevant data and information.

I acknowledge the role of the Institute of Criminology, headed by Professor Deosoran of the University of the West Indies at St. Augustine in Trinidad, whose greatest compliment to me was that I reminded him of himself in his early years. I must express my appreciation to Dean Deborah McPhee and Dr. Phyllis Scott, as well as to Professor Sharon Singleton and Walter Pierce of Barry University School of Social Work in Miami Shores, Florida, who provided me with the support and the opportunity to look at comparative models of violence intervention and prevention in the South Florida region of the United States. This exposure was invaluable in developing alternative models that can be utilized in the Caribbean.

The publication would not have come to fruition without the tireless efforts of Mrs. Yvonne Wallace and Mrs. Monica Tomlinson, whose persistence and meticulous attention to detail transformed my hieroglyphics, the children's drawings, charts, photographs and text into a readable document. Their contribution to this particular publication is priceless, and I will be forever indebted to them for their work on it.

My family has been intimately involved throughout this publication, and I must thank my husband, Omar Sr. and my daughters Nicole and Janelle for their support with editing the manuscript and transporting the children's drawings back and forth across the Caribbean. Thanks to my son, Omar Jr., my parents, siblings Sheryll, Perry and Harold, and their families, for their prayers, constant encouragement as well as motivation to get the project finished, particularly in the final stages when I was experiencing seemingly insurmountable physical and other challenges in a foreign land.

It is interesting to note that this undertaking has contributed to my own spiritual development.

I cannot end without expressing my appreciation to the children and their families who allowed me into their lives. It is my fervent hope that the presentation and analysis of their stories will be of some benefit to other children throughout the Caribbean and the Diaspora.

THE IMPACT OF GLOBALIZATION
on Caribbean Child Welfare

O N E could argue that the global impact of violence generally, and youth violence in particular, is one of the most serious, and consequently, one of the most topical social public health problems to emerge within the last two decades. The nature of this violence has been so severe and far-reaching in terms of its impact on victims, their families and their communities, that it has become a social problem of concern to almost every society in the world.

In recent years the issue of violence as it relates to terrorism (as a contributor to the overall problem of violence) has overshadowed the fact that individual small states such as those in the Caribbean have serious concerns with the regional problems associated with violence, which in and of themselves are of serious concern to the Caribbean basin region. In Jamaica, much of the violence manifests itself as criminal activity, the scale and scope of which have almost paralyzed law enforcement officials, social scientists, as well as social planners, in terms of their ability to analyze the etiology and nature of the problem, and to come up with effective solutions.

As the scourge of violence sweeps across the globe and the region increasingly, Caribbean social scientists have had to grapple with questions relating to the anatomy of violence in the region (that is, the how, and the why, of violence), in order to come up with the answers which their societies expect them to provide. One of the important questions that must be addressed by these professionals is: What are the factors that make the islands of the Caribbean susceptible to the high levels of crime and violence they are currently experiencing?

Though there are many theories as to the causes of violence and its consequences globally, much of the discussions have focused on violence in terms of the role of youth as perpetrators. Increasingly in the Caribbean, however, there is evidence that the characteristics and nature of violence in contemporary society is different in many respects from other parts of the world, particularly in terms of the extent to which violence involves children as victims and to some extent as perpetrators. There is need to analyse, therefore, the two-pronged nature of this violence, as well as its impact and etiology on the general socialization of the children who live with ongoing trauma and violence in their families and in their communities. This analysis has implications for the role of the primary agencies of socialization, which include the family, the media, and the community (including the school and church), as the re-socialization of children exposed to violence through these key agencies of socialization is essential to any violence prevention strategy. Other characteristics of Caribbean society which increases its vulnerability are geographic factors as well as social and economic factors.

Photo 1: The school system has an important role to play in the re-socialization of children exposed to violence. Here children in one urban Jamaican school recite the anger pledge as part of a school-wide behaviour change mentorship programme – "The Behaviour Hype Zone", developed by the author.

Geographic Vulnerability

Given the impact of globalization on international travel and trade, there has been a strengthening of social and economic linkages between the developed and the developing world which has led to greater risks for small vulnerable island states like those in the Caribbean. In the past, these islands have historically been an important centerpiece of the triangular slave trade route which involved trade in human cargo in the form of African slaves for sugar, manufactured goods and arms. As pirates of that period plundered the ships that plied these routes, the islands of the Caribbean became infamous as locations for illicit trading activities. In contemporary Caribbean society this trend has continued into the 21st century with the international drug trade, as well as trade in criminalized commodities such as weapons creating a background for unprecedented levels of crime and violence in the small island developing states that make up the Caribbean basin.

From Jamaica in the north to Guyana in the south, violent crime has been on the increase, even in the tiny islands of St. Kitts and Nevis, St. Lucia, Guadeloupe and Dominica where, for example, anecdotal reports from parents suggest that the problem of human trafficking, as evidenced by the illegal migration of children for adoption, using well developed criminal networks, have become new ways in which children's lives are being affected by violence.[1] Recent newspaper reports regarding isolated cases of child kidnapping out of Trinidad and Tobago also add to concerns regarding these claims (*Trinidad Guardian* February 2009).

Ideal transshipment ports

The reality of contemporary Caribbean society, therefore, is that: (i) there is ease of travel and communication which arise from the strategic location of the islands; (ii) the inefficiency and/or the inability of regional governments to use national resources to support the economies of these islands; and (iii) there are inadequate human and material resources needed to monitor and patrol their difficult borders, placing the islands of the region in the unenviable geographic position of being ideal transshipment ports for all types of illicit criminal activities, including the international drug trade and the illegal

---

1 Focus group discussions held with parents - Guadeloupe Parenting Partners 2004. (Interviews conducted by Parenting Partners of Jamaica)

weapons trade.[2] The fact that there are limited resources (human and material) to combat this level of criminal activity is therefore at the centre-piece of the issues that have fuelled, and continue to fuel the fire of violence in these island states, particularly in some of the larger Caribbean nations like Jamaica and Trinidad and Tobago.

The impact of natural disasters

The impact of natural disasters, which wreak havoc indiscriminately on the economies of small island developing states on a regular basis year after year, is one area that has micro and macro social and economic implications for Caribbean territories as individual small states, and for the region as a whole. Under-resourced island states are hard-pressed to find material and other resources to meet the needs of children and families who are forced to flee from the natural disasters which claim their homes on a regular basis. Though much has been done at a local and regional level to ameliorate the difficulties experienced by children and families caused by disasters such as hurricanes in particular, the reality of Caribbean lifestyles is that storms and hurricanes are as much a part of the national lifestyle as are the associated difficulties. In Jamaica, as shown in the drawing below, some children associate storms and hurricanes, for example, with looting and gun violence.

Underutilization of community shelters for children and families

As shown in Illustration 1 below, one 8-year-old boy, when asked to depict the impact of a hurricane on himself and his family, depicted gun violence as part of his experience. In the drawing, apart from the image of mangoes and other fruits being torn from the trees, and zinc fences blowing in the wind, there is a clear illustration of gun violence in the foreground, with three men shooting at each other. This child expressed the view that he understood why his parents did not go to a shelter, and he had stayed with his father during Hurricane Ivan in 2004 to prevent criminals from looting his family's possessions. Here we see children placed at risk for a natural disaster because of the fear of violence against their homes perpetrated by community criminals. The result is a generation of children who associate rain and floods with criminals attacking their homes and their families,

---

2   Human Development Report 2006.

Illustration 1: An 8-year-old boy's drawing showing looting and shooting during a hurricane which affected his island home

and a generation of adults who are preoccupied with protecting their possessions from criminals, thereby not using government shelters, thus putting their children and other family members at risk.

A major issue of social vulnerability therefore, relates to the absence of a community culture which protects children from the worst forms of violence. This is preventable and relates to ineptitude on the part of the state in enforcing law and order at the community level during a natural disaster, as well as in normal community life. This is a problem that has existed in the tenure of both major political parties in Jamaica, and is one that must be addressed as part of long-term disaster preparedness planning, in collaboration with the Office of Disaster Preparedness and Emergency Management (ODPEM).

Economic Vulnerability

Apart from the issue of geographic vulnerability mentioned above, small island states within the Caribbean have always had unique social, political and economic challenges which make them extremely vulnerable to a variety of internal and external factors. This inherent vulnerability is based on factors such as the historical vestiges of slavery and colonialism, as well as other, more contemporary post-colonial issues such as economic policies related to the structural adjustment of local economies, and policies which are often dictated unilaterally for the most part by agencies such as the International Monetary Fund and other multi-lateral funding agencies. These agencies often prescribe policies which result in harsh socio-economic restrictions in exchange for important international financial stabilization protocols.

Other variables include income growth volatility due to a lack of economic diversification. This is related, but not confined, to high degrees of export dependence, low Gross Domestic Product (GDP) (see Table 1), debt-service ratios, as well as the socio-economic issues related to the impact of repeated natural disasters.

Social Vulnerability

Apart from the problems of geographic and economic vulnerability, there are also inherent social vulnerabilities that predispose children to violence in the Caribbean. These include changes in family values and culture that have led to community instability manifested as parenting inadequacies and the associated absence of the traditional cultural protections afforded to children. When this is compounded by the lack of attention of Caribbean governments to children's issues and the inherent vulnerability of the children themselves, we therefore find communities and, by extension, societies where children become increasingly at risk for violence in its different forms.

Impact of Globalization

Though globalization has its advantages in terms of the ease of the dissemination of technology, it has also made these small island states increasingly susceptible to the effects of this violence, by virtue of the social and economic vulnerabilities discussed above. There are also additional new problems that have been introduced as societies have become more interdependent. As stated by Kofi Annan, former Secretary General of the United Nations, these "problems have no passports" and have, therefore, become problems without borders. One of the most significant of these global problems with particular relevance to the Caribbean region is the international nature of criminal behaviour particularly with respect to drug and weapon trafficking within and between the region. These problems have had a tremendous impact on Caribbean society in terms of the social implications of these developments. Intricate and extensive criminal networks have emerged within these Caribbean states in small villages and communities. These networks have linked the small island developing states in the Caribbean to the major metropolitan criminal centres of the world, mainly in the United Kingdom, the United States and Canada.

These networks are well organized, very well funded, and often their net worth far surpasses the GDP of most of the countries in which they operate (see Appendix 1). One report suggested that the net worth of the illegal drugs passing through Jamaica in 2004, for example, was almost the size of the country's national budget.[3]

Vulnerability of Children Themselves

From an anthropological perspective, the human child has always been identified as being the most vulnerable of the animal species, taking 21 years to reach to adulthood, as against hours and days in the animal kingdom. The human child, therefore, in comparison with most other species in the animal kingdom, needs the most protection for the longest period, and is thus extremely vulnerable to predators and other forces in his/her environment which can cause harm. Historically, most societies spend much of their resources to protect their children, particularly the very young, as this is the time when they are most at risk of being harmed. The Caribbean, this text suggests, given its increased vulnerability to crime, has not committed sufficient resources to the protection of its children, and so, as a group, they are more vulnerable than children in many other developing societies which may not have the same geographic social or economic characteristics.

The Vulnerability Model

The model below graphically illustrates the relationship between the different levels and types of vulnerability in small island developing

---

3   Human Development Report (2006).

states in the Caribbean. It suggests that the development of violence
in these societies and the consequent risks posed to our children are
a result of historical and economic vulnerabilities, in addition to
geographic and social vulnerabilities as discussed above.

Chart 1: *The vulnerability model*

HISTORIC ECONOMIC VULNERABILTY (lack of resources for effective
and efficient social service delivery and law enforcement systems)

+

GEOGRAPHIC VULNERABILITY (weaponization of trade; ease of drug transshipment through the region; easy access to illegal weapons/preponderance of
natural disasters)

+

SOCIAL VULNERABILITY (family instability due to lack of effective
and efficient social safety nets and other protective systems
for children/culture of violence led by socioeconomic political forces)

+

VULNERABIITY OF CHILDREN THEMSELVES

= CHILDREN AT RISK FOR VIOLENCE

The model above suggests that notwithstanding the well
documented political genesis of violence in the Caribbean region the
problem of violence is partially linked to the notion of the vulnerability
of small states as it relates to the impact of globalization. As shown
in the vulnerability model, it is possible that the Caribbean islands
have an inherent vulnerability to economic instability and natural
disasters. It could be argued that the impact that this has had on their
tourism-driven economies, is fuelling the rise in crime rates across
the Caribbean, changing the pattern of crime, and causing increases
in more serious crimes. These factors are therefore symptoms of
the increased vulnerability of small island states to globalization in
terms of trade policies, as well as the changes related to operations
of global criminal networks, particularly with regard to the ease of
travel and communication.

The impact of increased criminal activity in these small island
states in particular, hits hardest at the most vulnerable in the society,
namely the elderly, the physically and mentally challenged, and most

significantly, the region's children. The following section summarizes some of the issues that children experience that are related to violence, and discusses the systemic inadequacies in the social welfare systems that are contributing to this problem.

Social Welfare and Social Development – Issues in the Caribbean

As mentioned previously, Jamaica's situation with respect to crime and violence has always been different from the rest of the Caribbean. However, the fact that violence is spreading so rapidly across societies previously thought to be less susceptible to violence than Jamaica, suggests that there are possible changes occurring in the value system of Caribbean society, fuelled primarily by the effects of globalization, which are in turn impacting on the primary agents of socialization, such as the family and the secondary agents of socialization such as, the media, and other cultural crossover variables, such as attitudes to women and children (Harriot 2000). Given Jamaica's central role as the cultural hub of the Caribbean, it is not surprising that the changes in values and mores and ethics relating to parenting and child-rearing which are emerging out of that country, are rapidly spreading across the Caribbean. This therefore could be one of the factors at the micro level and at the level of the community and society, which has created in an incubator for the changes in attitudes towards violence generally and towards children in particular.

This text argues that violence affecting children in the Caribbean results from a combination of factors that arise primarily from the effects of globalization and the accompanying social and economic vulnerabilities of the region as a whole. It suggests that, in addition, there are inherent challenges facing the under-resourced social agencies serving children, adolescents and their families. The violence persists and has become more visible, given the fact that children in any society are the most vulnerable to the effects of poverty. They are also most at risk as a result of the mezzo, community-based as well as macro social and economic changes occuring in their societies by virtue of their position at the bottom of the economic ladder. It is not surprising therefore that there has been a shift in the pattern of criminal behaviour, where Caribbean children are the ones who are increasingly becoming perpetrators of violence, as well as its victims, in some instances being targeted in a premeditated manner by some criminals.

Changes in patterns of criminal behaviour in the Caribbean

The above discussion suggests that across the Caribbean it appears that the scourge of violence is not only spreading in terms of the prevalence of violent crime, but there are specific patterns in the nature of crime, particularly regarding its relation to the impact on children and younger adolescents that are cause for some concern. These patterns seem to be at variance with the traditional cultural mores and values associated with Caribbean culture and lifestyles to the extent that children are involved as victims and as perpetrators.

Caribbean islands are more than beaches

The Caribbean has long been seen across the world as being the playground of the rich and famous. Consequently, for decades, there has been a global perception, oftentimes held by Caribbean peoples themselves, that these tiny island states, which make up the archipelago of the Caribbean, were immune to the social problems of the wealthier nations in the metropolitan north. This resulted for many years in colonial and post-colonial governments of the region ignoring or not paying sufficient attention to these social problems. It was only after the emphasis on social development by Norman Manley in Jamaica and Eric Williams in Trinidad in the 1940s and '50s that governments of the Caribbean started to focus in a very rudimentary way on state provisions of social services.

As Caribbean societies developed into the 21st century with the high youth dependency ratios created bulging youth populations, few Caribbean societies realized the need to re-tool their human resource resources in terms of the training of social workers and counselling professionals and other social practitioners in particular, in order to provide ameliorative social services for the new demands and challenges of the 21st century.

Only in the past two decades has there been some attention paid to social development, and then mainly on education and health, with, for many years, a reduced focus on family and child welfare (Crawford-Brown 1998). The economists of the day have argued consistently that social development is only possible when there is economic development to pay for social services. As a result, the coffers of most social service and social welfare agencies have had to wait for budgetary allocations for years in order to provide the basic human and material resources to deal with family support services, school support services, child and family protection and support services. Looking at Trinidad and Tobago, the profits earned by the oil boom are the sole means fuelling their ability to implement a comparatively greater number of the human resources needed to address the serious social problems in its schools and communities. These resources include increased numbers of social workers in the educational system, as well as mental health officers and community development and youth workers at the community level.

Gaps in policy development versus operationalization of services

In Jamaica there are also gaps between macro policy initiatives and the operationalization of these policies. The post of a social worker at the only children's hospital in Jamaica has been unfilled for years, despite the fact that a sign was placed designating a room for this position since the hospital was built in the 1960s. More recently, a cadre of well-trained social workers have been put into place in the school system in Trinidad and Tobago, giving guidance counsellors in that twin island state an opportunity to work holistically with children with emotional, behavioural and learning problems within the school system. In one social commentary regarding the recent murder of a six year boy by early adolescent boys in Trinidad and Tobago, one newspaper commentator queried whether it was too little too late.

Socio-cultural changes in the family

The argument that could be made is that, while the Caribbean struggled to catch up economically to be able to afford adequate or basic social services, there has been massive social change at the level of the community and family due to globalization and other social and economic factors, resulting in migration and return migration flows into and out of the Caribbean. Though these migration flows have facilitated the movement of much needed expertise to and from the region, with the transfer of technology and new and exciting cultural practices from the metropole to these postcolonial societies, return migration has come with changes in the traditional values and mores of the Caribbean people. Without well developed safety nets and safeguards in the human service systems, under-girded by effective administration and policy development frameworks for these social services, and without the necessary resources to reinforce values, provide checks and balances in the homes, schools and communities, this text argues that there has been a gradual deterioration in the traditional family values which have been the mainstay of Caribbean culture for generations.

Cultural pluralism

Given the cultural pluralism of Caribbean societies with its changing and dynamic melting pot of sub-cultures, there has been for decades a free-for-all situation with respect to the maintenance of the basic values regarding family and community that make up these societies. Without adequate and strong administrations in the social service structures, there has been a breakup in the social fabric of many of traditional Caribbean societies. These societies are no longer protected by the informal social control mechanism of communal living and no longer dependent on the role of the elderly, and other legacies of African societies which have served the region well as alternatives to the more formal social service structures. As modernity and development have moved across the Caribbean, the lack of a system for adequate protection of children in particular has therefore fallen by the wayside, forgotten in the rush to develop our economies and to keep up with rapidly changing social, economic and political activities. The reality is, however, that as the Caribbean societies move to become more developed, it has to be recognized that checks and balances in the social services are an integral part of the administration of a more developed society. These services must be policed by an institutionalized child welfare system one which has to be integrated into the educational system.

Neglect of child welfare policies

Years of neglect of child welfare policies in the Caribbean has created a situation where Caribbean social service systems have adopted a laissez-faire approach with respect to the protection of children and by extension childhood. In addition, there has been an accompanying lack of attention to the importance of child protection and early intervention, particularly for emotion and behavioural issues. Given the global impact of institutionalized crime in the region, Caribbean children have therefore been one of the most vulnerable groups which have been excluded by social policy intervention and left out in the cold, despite the natural love that our people have for their children. The result is that our child victims of violence, like other excluded children in the Child Welfare System, are now reaping the consequences of years of neglected social welfare and child welfare structures and policies which should have been set in place to protect them and to cater to their welfare.

Child protection issues

During this time, issues such as effective assessment and intervention policies to address the physical and sexual abuse of children were allowed to get out of control. The result was that several generations of Caribbean peoples have grown up in cultures where child abuse, particularly sexual abuse, has bee viewed as part of the "social fabric" of child-rearing practice and as an issue that should be kept secret and swept under the proverbial carpet of family and community relationships (Crawford-Brown 2000).

Summary

This chapter suggests that the violence in Jamaica comes from the inherent vulnerability of Caribbean societies, based on historical, geographic, social and economic factors. In addition, the violence that is presently impacting on our children is a symptom of a pattern of criminal behaviour that has changed over the past two decades such that there is much more group and community involvement in the form of criminal gangs. In his discussion of the behaviour of gangs, one theorist suggests that the concept of a social identity in a gang becomes such that any action against one member becomes an action against all, and this therefore legitimizes much of violent criminal gang activities (Harriott 2000).

This also happens because family members are expected to take responsibility for the action of each family member (Harriott 2003). When these family members are children, the children, Harriott suggests, become soft targets and a pattern of children as victims has developed, where, for example, child murder is associated for the most part with reprisals for various criminal or social squabbles that have not been resolved by the adult relatives.

Figure 1: *Number of children murdered over the years 2000-2005*

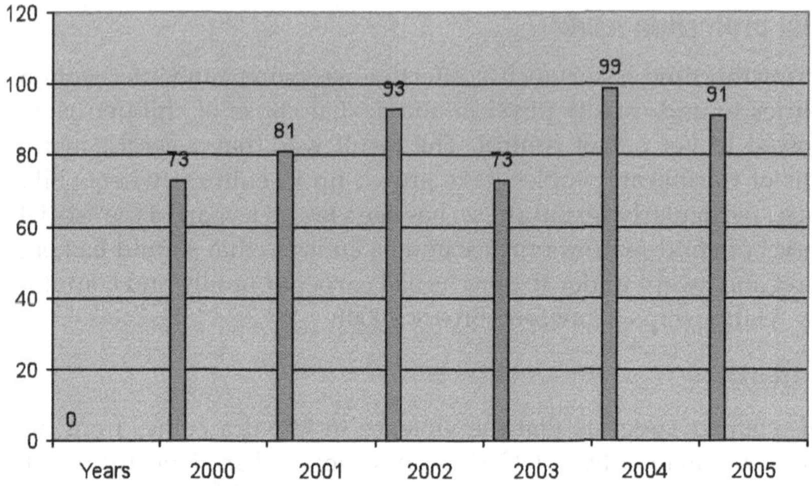

This chapter has therefore traced patterns of violence from their global and regional significance and shown that the patterns of violence directed against children, seen in Jamaica, are part of an escalation of a specific type of criminal behaviour possibly linked to the development of gangs which is in turn linked to the escalation of drugs and weapons trading in the region. This is possible because of the vulnerability of small states like Jamaica to social and economic deficiencies.

Naivety of Caribbean society

This text suggests that neglect, apathy and the suddenness of the impact of globalization have caught most Caribbean governments and societies with their proverbial "pants down" and, with some amount of naivety, these societies have not prepared themselves adequately for the challenges of the 21st century in the new era of globalization particularly as it relates to the provision of an all-important safety net for the most vulnerable sectors of its population. It is therefore up to the governments and the technocrats at regional and national levels to integrate their human resources to more adequately meet these new and monumental challenges. Fighting these major issues singly as island states as we have been doing for decades cannot adequately address the problems.

Role of CARICOM

Given the advent of the CARICOM Single Market Economy (CSME), the time is ripe for the development of creative solutions, using regional consultative mechanisms, for dealing with these issues. The content of this book is therefore meant to be used as the framework for such a creative response. Failure to address these issues in a timely fashion by understanding what faces us and by developing the effective solutions to address the serious issues highlighted, will be to our peril, as individual societies, and as a region.

CHAPTER ONE

VIOLENCE AFFECTING
Children as Victims

T H E issue of violent crime is one of the biggest, if not the biggest challenge, facing the people of Jamaica. As discussed in the Introduction, though the problem of violence and crime is a global phenomenon, there are features of violent crime in the Caribbean which make it particularly challenging and of great concern to social planners, practitioners and the population in general. The key feature in the Caribbean is the extent to which children are the victims and the perpetrators of violent crime, as well as being witnesses to various forms of violence. This chapter will look at the issue of children as victims of violence. in terms of (a) the nature of violence generally; (b) child murder; (c) sexual violence; and (d) the kidnapping and abduction of children.

The Nature of Violence Affecting Children as Victims

In 2004 more than four persons were victims of murder (the most extreme form of interpersonal violence) each day in Jamaica. Of that total, 119 were children. In 2005 1,347 persons were murdered in Jamaica, 105 of that number being children. These figures remain similar through to 2009, with abductions and kidnappings being added to the list of motives, particularly since 2007. Many children become victims when they are exposed to traumatic events directly, by being victims themselves, when they are witnesses to violent crimes (through face to face interaction or through the media), or when they are at risk for violence. Children experience therefore, a range of violent experiences in their homes, schools as well as in their communities.

Children as victims of violence can be grouped into three categories: (i) children who are directly involved; (ii) children who are indirectly involved; and (iii) children who are at risk for violence by virtue of their lifestyle or life circumstances.

The table below shows that children who are **classified as being directly involved as victims of violence** are in a wide range of circumstances. These are children exposed to situations where they may be physically, emotionally, or verbally abused. Children in this category are also victims of sexual abuse. Other children who are directly involved as victims of violence, may be victims of fire as a result of poor living conditions, e.g. drowning as a result of lack of supervision at school or in their communities. Some of these children may become prostitutes putting themselves at risk for direct violent acts, also as a result of lack of supervision or poor parenting.

Table 1: *Children as victims of all forms of violence*

Level of Involvement	Description of Circumstance
Directly involved	Victims of sexual violence, emotional violence or physical violence, e.g. victims of murder, victims of injury, (shootings, stabbings in school, home or community), victims of traffic accidents, drowning, fire, suicide, lightning. Children involved in prostitution voluntarily with/without parental consent.
Indirectly involved	Children in violence prone communities are susceptible to all of the above forms of direct violence as witnesses e.g. to sexual violence, to non-fatal shootings, physical beatings, to murder and other violence in the home, school, community, as well as other forms of violence transmitted through the media. Unsuspecting children talking to reporters about what they have seen put them at risk for retaliatory violence. These children need sensitization and protection.

Children at risk	Abused children, children with disabilities, childrend of migration, street and working children, children in alternative parenting situations, inadequately supervised children, children living in volatile urban communities, children mentored by gang members with/or without parental consent, children on school trips without adequate supervision, children in schools with school personnel unable to swim, inadequate training in crisis management and basic first aid, children in state care.

Children who are **classified as being indirectly involved** are those who are witnesses to violence. These children often live in violence-prone communities. Many of them may be also directly involved in violent acts, as discussed above. But, in addition, witness sexual violence, fatal and non-fatal shootings, as well as murder in all situations in which they are socialized. These include their homes, schools and communities. These witnesses can also be described as groups of children who are exposed to violence in the media or lewd music. This type of music is often played at community dances and on public transportation. Another threat to children who are witnesses to violence comes from their exposure to pornographic movies and other materials accessible to them through the illegal operators within the transportation system.

Children at risk are described as children who have not yet become victims or witnesses, but live in difficult circumstances, where they may become directly involved or may witness violence. These are children who need preventive intervention and include children who are living and working on the streets, who may be abused by older adolescents and young adult street workers. Children with disabilities are particularly susceptible to violence because of a sub-cultural attitude to the disabled who may be physically or mentally challenged. Those children who are living in alternative parenting situations include children in state institutions and children in foster care. Though these systems are set up to protect children, the reality is that they are often at risk for violence from the employees of institutions, many of whom are untrained, and abuse them rather than protect them (Crawford-Brown 1989). Children are at risk for violence in schools as a result of corporal punishment, inadequate supervision while on school trips, and children who are not supervised before and after school.

General crimes affecting children

Of the total number of children who die violently in Jamaica each year, the largest number of them died by traffic accidents up to 1999. Other factors causing the violent death of children, for example, included in 1996, drowning 5, suicide 2, death by fire 6, and lightning 1. In 1996, 6 children were murdered. It is important to note that in 1998, the number of children who were murdered increased to the point of surpassing the number of children who died by traffic accidents (see Appendix II).

School-based violence

Newspaper editorials and media reports over the past decades also speak to the frightening increase in violence in schools, with resulting apathy and fear by teachers towards their students, and a disquiet and anxiety in some children, as they make their way to and from school. The presence of school-based violence in both urban and rural communities speaks to the pervasive nature of the different forms of violence affecting children. Though Jamaica has yet to see the more extreme forms of school-based gang violence currently being experienced in big urban centres of the United States, such as in the Chicago school system, it must be acknowledged that the Jamaican school is the community context within which some of the violence against children takes place. This violence affects them most seriously as they make their way to or from school, when they may be victims of abductions or traffic accidents, or when they use the transportation system. The transportation system for school children, or "school-ers" as they are colloquially called, which had been structured just a decade ago with designated school buses, has deteriorated to the point where child predators use the transportation system to expose unwilling and sometimes willing minors to inappropriate sexual activity.

Within the school system, however, some of the violence occurs as a result of corporal punishment. Other forms of violence to which children may be exposed in school include, principally, interpersonal fighting, which may or may not occasion physical assault resulting in bodily injury. Despite a plethora of programmes instituted by the state, such as PALS (Peace and Love in Schools), and PASS (Programme for Alternate School Support), which have made some inroads into the values and attitudes related to violence, and other attempts to provide some innovations by individual schools such as the Change from Within Project, the state, so far, has been unable to significantly reduce the incidence of violence in schools. This is primarily due to the lack of an integrating framework and ineffective referral systems within the schools to allow for rapid assessment and intervention with children who are the victims and perpetrators of violence. The Jamaica society has therefore been unable to keep its children safe in one of the most important agencies of socialization.

Community-based violence

Violence in various forms has therefore been taking a heavy toll on the physical and mental health of Jamaican children, with children exhibiting symptoms of depression, post-traumatic stress disorder, aggressive and impulsive behaviours, difficulty concentrating, bedwetting, attachment problems, many of the symptoms existing within the context of unstable familial environments. These are all are factors that are associated with aggressive and delinquent behaviours (Samms-Vaughn 2005), further fuelling our present epidemic of violence. A study by the Ministry of Health in Kingston and St. Andrew concluded that 25% of adolescents do not feel 100% safe in their communities, and 30% of these adolescents in Jamaica stated that they worry about fighting and violence in their homes, schools and communities.[4] This could also be due to the fact that too many children are the victims of very serious and vicious crimes and their anxiety is grounded in the reality of their experience.

Vicious crimes

As shown in Figure 2, in 2001, the total number of child victims of vicious crimes, which included murders, shootings, rape/carnal abuse, as well as robbery and break-ins into their family home, was 1,081. These were child victims between the ages of 0-18. It is important to note that, the children who were victims of rape and carnal abuse were by far the largest group (504), while murder (80), robbery (80) and shootings (82) were highly significant, and the cause of much concern. The disproportionate nature of the rape and carnal

---

4   UNICEF, *Violence Against Children in the Caribbean Region: Regional Report* (UNICEF 2005).

Figure 2: *Major crimes committed against youth 18 years and under in Jamaica 2001*

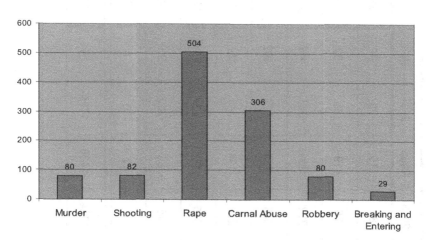

Source: Planning Institute of Jamaica, *A report of the Social Indicators Monitoring System* (UNICEF/PIOJ, 2005)

abuse rates where children are victims is worthy of note, and will be discussed later in this chapter. Though these data date back to 2001 as shown in the Table 2, the incidence of children who were victims of vicious crimes has increased steadily up to 2008, from a total of 728 cases in 2001 to 960 cases in 2004, and 1,571 cases in 2008.

It is important to note that in looking at these data that prior to the 1970s, there was relatively little historical precedent for a pattern of criminal behaviour which deliberately targeted children particularly as it related to murder, abductions and kidnappings. The sections in this chapter will now discuss on three major forms of violence affecting children in Jamaica, namely (1) children as victims of murder; (2) children as victims of sexual violence; and (3) children as victims of kidnapping and abduction. These issues were highlighted as there appears to be a sense of urgency in the society to understand these phenomena, which were previously unknown in Jamaica and the rest of the Caribbean just over a decade ago.

Children as Victims of Murder

In looking at children as victims of murder in 2005, over 100 Jamaican children were victims of the most extreme form of violence against a person – murder. In that same year, 463 children and youth between

Table 2: *Offences against children between the ages of 0-15 – 2000-2004*.

OFFENCES	2000	2001	2002	2003	2004	2005	2006	2007	2008	Total
Murder	5	13	17	13	16	89	65	70	94	382
Shooting	20	33	33	37	42	75	19	71	62	392
Rape	147	303	326	360	358	382	351	348	449	3024
Carnal Abuse	434	306	270	377	409	346	434	427	462	3465
Wounding	20	28	20	34	40	258	194	245	156	995
Assault	58	38	48	52	55	525	327	409	315	1827
Abduction	11	7	10	19	39	45	38	200	33	402
Abandonment of Child	8	0	1	1	1	4	2	5	0	22
Total	703	728	725	893	960	1724	1430	1775	1571	10509

Source: Statistical Institute- Kingston, Jamaica

0-24 years were murdered, compared to 327 in 2001.[5] The deliberate killing of children in any society that is not at war is an unnatural activity, therefore making these rates unnerving and of some concern to social planners and practitioners as it suggests a disturbing trend. It is important, therefore, to look at the motives behind these seemingly unusual acts.

Motives for murder of children

As discussed earlier in this chapter, it was during the 1990s that social analysts began to see a major change in the pattern of criminal activities where, for the first time, there appeared to be a significant number of criminal acts that were specifically directed at children.

Data on the motives for the murder of children show that the motives for the majority of the children murdered in Jamaica in 2001 were classified as being related to domestic issues. The second biggest motive for the murder of children was related to gangs and reprisal killings.[6] These figures are of much concern as the data beg the question as to the nature and effectiveness of socialization agencies which breed those who can so easily murder children. The data also suggest that there is tremendous need to do an in-depth and comprehensive investigation into this problem, as the national data suggest that children have become prime targets in adult battles. This goes against the grain of traditional Caribbean culture.

Motives as deliberate acts

The data suggest therefore that, whereas earlier murders of children were usually non-deliberate, by the late nineties, as shown in Figure 3, between 1998 and 2001 the motives for the killing of children show premeditation, with domestic disputes being the biggest contributing factor. It is interesting to note that between 2001 and 2005 as shown in Figure 4 below, community based murders (grouped as gang reprisals, rape outside of the home, and other criminal acts) seemed to assume pre-eminence with domestic factors becoming secondary. It could be argued that community criminals took their cues from the family while the state and the rest of civil society watched helplessly.

---

5 Office of the Prime Minister, Social Policy Initiative: Juvenile Justice Reform (2006).

6 Constabulary Communications Network (CCN) 2002.

Figure 3: *Motives for killing children in Jamaica 1998-2001*

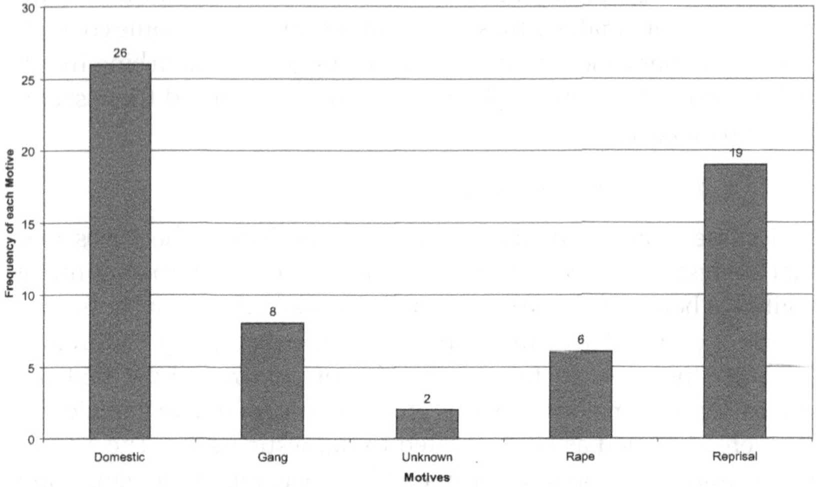

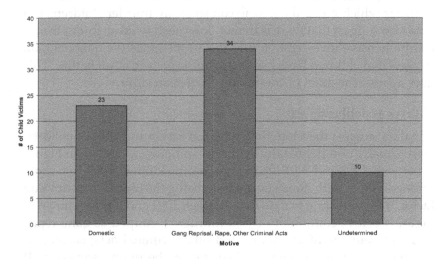

Figure 4: *Motives underlying murder of children in Jamaica 2001-2005*

This is an area that could be investigated more thoroughly through empirical research using case studies.

According to police statistics, and as shown in Figure 5, the main factors that resulted in children dying violently between 1996 and 1997 included traffic accidents, murder, drowning, fire and lightning, with traffic accidents in that period being the factor causing the greatest number of children's deaths (34) versus murder, which at

Figure 5: *Incidents of children killed violently by cause of death (1996-1997) in Jamaica*

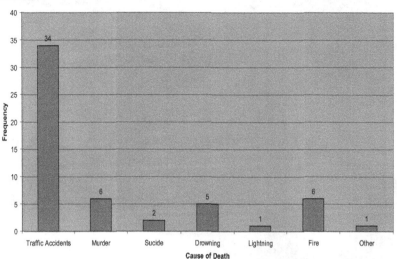

Figure 6: *Incidents of children killed violently by cause of death (1998-2001) in Jamaica*

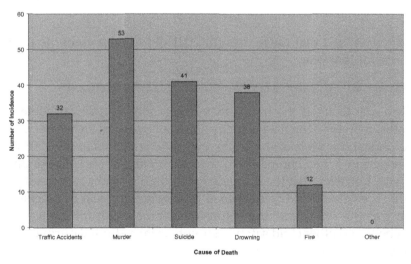

the time claimed the lives of 6 children, up from 2 children the year before. As shown in Figure 6, between 1998 and 2001, the figures changed dramatically, with 53 children murdered over the three-year period, and a much smaller number of children (32) dying as a result of traffic accidents, than was recorded in 1996 (34 for a single year).

Photo 2: Children in the "Peace Warrior" programme

It is to be noted that the figures for 2001 did not represent the total figures for that year.

Increase in child murders, decrease in traffic accidents

When one looks at the trends in terms of all categories of violent deaths, therefore, the data actually show an overall increase in child murders and a decrease in deaths by traffic accidents in the 1998 to 2001 period, when compared to the year 1996-1997. It is important to note, however, that the decrease in children's deaths as a result of traffic accidents could be explained by the fact that seat belt legislation was put into place and enforcement procedures for the use of seat belts and other child safety restraints were instituted during that time.

Children as "soft targets"

The ruthlessness of criminals who go after children because they are "soft targets" and easily accessible both as kidnap and murder victims, and the increased complexity of the crimes, coupled with the internationalization of the crimes themselves have hardened

Illustration 2: A child's drawing to show children stopping to allow a car to pass – practising road safety (Road Safety is an important preventive strategy to decrease child fatalities.)

the landscape of criminal behaviour, cutting through the traditional cultural patterns which had traditionally put women, children and the elderly outside of the realm of criminal activity. When one examines the much talked about decrease in property crimes in Jamaica[7] the data suggest that for the years 2001-2005, there was actually a decrease in property crimes. However, more serious crimes such as extortion and murder increased over the same period and therefore increases in crimes against business places and a growth in extortion practices at the community level. Criminal behaviour patterns involving extortion have not been a common type of crime found in most small island states in the Caribbean.[8] Increasing trends in this direction are therefore worrying to social planners as they have a direct impact on the economic and investment climate on small island economies and suggest that this may have developed from a lack of attention to the problem of bullying and extortion behaviour in the school system where children are victims first and may become perpetrators later.

---

7   Human Development Report (2006).
8   Ibid.

Weapons used against children

One of the more disturbing features of violence against children and their families in Jamaica relates to the methods used to harm children. When one examines the data which show the weapons used in the murder of children (Figure 7), there is a wide range of weapons; these range from the more sensational but isolated case of an ice pick in one instance, to the more "common" weapons such as the gun. The large amount of weapons described as "other" suggested that perpetrators used any means at their disposal to murder their child victims, given the innate vulnerability of children. This data emphasized the need to strengthen the existing child protection legislation through monitoring and enforcement of child protection laws, as well as improved tracking mechanisms once children are abducted. The "Ananda Alert" legislation initiated in 2008 started this process.

Age groups of children affected

Children under five most vulnerable

The fact that children under 18 are being murdered is particularly worrying, and so are the figures on the rape of children under 18, where more than 60% of the total number of rape victims in 2001 were children under 18, while more than 50% of those were under 15 years. This data reflect the inherent vulnerability of children and the fact that they make easy targets.

As shown in Figure 2 (p. 21), all children under 18 years are affected by violence, but in looking at children who have been killed violently, that is, children who have been murdered, killed in accidents, as well as children killed in fires, the biggest group of children in this category was under age five.[9] This means that when we look at all children dying violently, it is the youngest and most vulnerable group of children who are at risk of being in harm's way.

Murder victims – rural/urban differentials

Urban life is often seen as a barometer of the worst excesses of violence in many societies. It is important therefore to look at the data across the country in the rural areas to get an accurate picture of how pervasive the problem of child murder is.

As shown in Figure 8 below, a total of 80 children were murdered island wide in 2001. It is important to note that of the 80 murders more

---

9   Constabulary Communications Network (CCN).

Figure 7: *Weapons used in the murder of children*

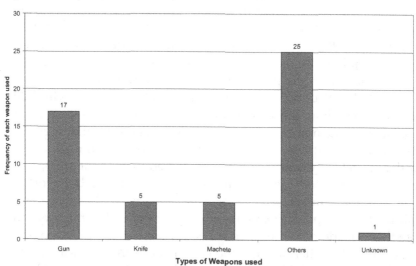

Photo 3: Children under five are most vulnerable

Photo 3*:* Children under five are most vulnerable

than half of them took place in the Kingston Metropolitan Region (57.5%), while 15% of these murders occurred in the neighbouring parish of St. Catherine. It is significant that the figures for that parish include the bustling suburban centres of Portmore (which has recently acquired city status), and Spanish Town (a densely populated town teeming with the problems of any modern urban centre). It is to be noted that data for shootings and robberies where children were victims follow the same pattern as murders where there are a disproportionate number of cases in the urban and suburban centres in comparison with the rural areas. In terms of the rural situation, Portland, Trelawny and Hanover, considered deep rural areas, had the lowest recorded cases of murder and shootings, but worthy of note is the number of cases of rape and carnal abuse affecting children in these parishes (see Figure 2, p. 21). It is also important to note that outside of the urban centres of the Kingston Metropolitan Region and St. Catherine, rape and carnal abuse are significant areas of violence against children. This specific issue will be discussed later in this chapter.

Gender differentials – victims of murder and shootings

As shown below, of the total child victims of murders in 2001, 84.8% were male and 15.2% were female.

It is important to note that there are major gender differentials in the data as they relate to victims of violence. As shown in Figure 9 below, in 2001 males were much more at risk for being victims than

Figure 8: *Number of murders of youth 18 years and under by parish 2001 (Jamaica)*

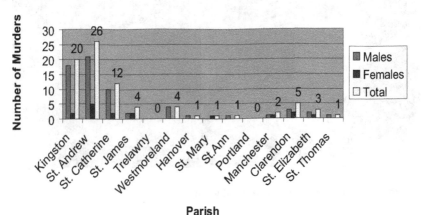

Parish

their female counterparts, particularly as it related to murder and shootings.

Children as Victims of Sexual Violence

The reporting dilemma – tip of the iceberg

As shown in Figure 2 (p. 21), there were a total of 504 incidents in 2001 island wide where children were victims of sexual violence, specifically rape. These incidents as shown in the Figure were disproportionately greater than any of the other offences against children. This issue will now be discussed in more detail.

Sexual crimes committed against children by adults, and by children on other children, have continued apace without any signs of significant reduction in the numbers over the years. In 2005, there were 367 cases of rape and carnal abuse reported. It is important to note that the reported cases in any country represent the tip of the proverbial iceberg, so that when one looks at the pattern of reporting, one set of research findings[10] found that whereas 85% of other crimes were reported, when the crime was rape, only 20% of this crime was reported in the sample studied. If these figures were to be used as an

Figure 9: *Children as victims of violence by gender 2001*

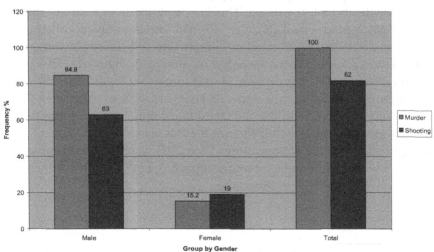

---

10 Task Force on Educational Reform. Final Report (Government of Jamaica, 2004).

index of reporting rates, it would mean that 1,800 cases of child rape may have occurred.[11] This contrasts with the 387 that were actually reported. In looking at the pattern of these crimes in terms of the involvement of children, some very significant trends emerge which are worthy of mention.

All forms of abuse have been of concern in Jamaica for some time, but sexual abuse is particularly troubling when one looks at the data on rape victims across all age groups. In fact, in an August 2006 media report, the Jamaican Minister of National Security made a point of commenting on the worrying fact that though the murder rate had decreased slightly when compared with the same period the year before, there were massive increases in the cases of carnal abuse over the same period in a scenario where these rates were already high.[12]

Gender differentials – victims of rape and carnal abuse

Sexual violence perpetuated against children remains, therefore, one of the most prevalent forms of child abuse in Jamaica. This is reflected in the fact that rape and carnal abuse is a significant area of violence affecting children and families. When one examines the data on the ages of the victims of rape in 2002, as shown in Figure 10 below, it is interesting to note that there are a disproportionate number of victims who are in the younger age groups when compared to older adolescents and adult women. This is symptomatic of a society that has long accepted sexual abuse as "normal" and has only recently put into place legislation for mandatory reporting and the establishment of a national Child Abuse Registry. As shown in Figure 11, 75% of rape victims in 2002 were under 25. It is important to note that when one examines those victims under 25 years old, 55% of them were 17 years and younger, with the children 14 and under representing the largest group of rape victims (Figure 10). It is also worthy of note that a significant number of boys under 18 in 2002 were victims of carnal abuse, but there is significant under-reporting of this information.

---

11 UNICEF, *Situation Analysis of Women and Children in Jamaica* (update/ 2006).

12 "Recent statistics from the Jamaica Constabulary Force showed that the incidence of adults, particularly males, having sexual relations with minors has increased by 31% over a five-year period" (*The Daily Gleaner*, August 25, 2006).

Figure 10: Children as victims of carnal abuse and rape by age group and gender 2002

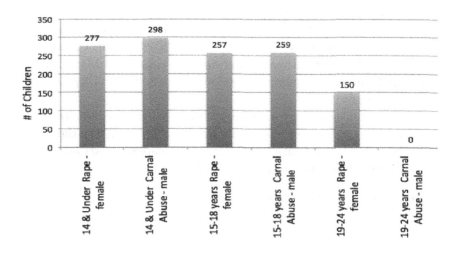

Figure 11: *Ages of victims of rape by percentage 2002*

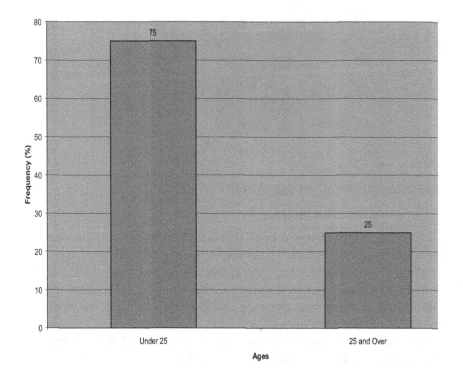

Rape and carnal abuse – rural/urban differentials

The parishes with the highest number of child victims of rape were St. Andrew, followed by Kingston and then St. Catherine.

As seen in Figure 12, cases of rape of children in 2002 were St. Andrew (25.5%), followed by Kingston (15.5%) and St. Catherine (11.5%). It is to be noted that Clarendon, St. James and Manchester recorded the highest number of rapes outside of Kingston, St. Andrew and St. Catherine.

Sexual violence perpetrated against children therefore remains one of the most prevalent forms of child abuse in Jamaica. The data on child abuse have raised various concerns for decades (Child Guidance Clinic Report 1986; Crawford-Brown 1999).

Figure 12: *Sexual violence by parish 2002 (Jamaica)*

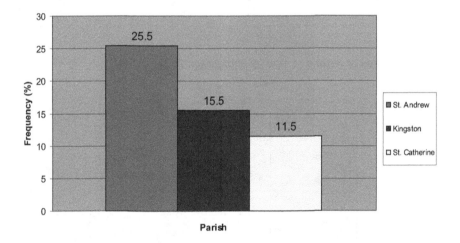

New dimensions of sexual violence

Male victims of sexual violence

The real incidence of young boys who are victims has not historically been reflected in the data. However, it is possible that these figures do not truly reflect the actual prevalence due to the stigma associated with homosexual acts in Jamaica. Child Welfare authorities must take this into account if they are to effectively address the special problems of this population.

Although much information on the prevalence of adult females abusing male children is anecdotal (McGill & Leiba, *The Daily Gleaner*

Illustration 3: "I am not her man, I am her son." The 8-year-old boy (Primary School, Kingston 4) who illustrated this picture brings to the forefront of public consciousness a relatively new phenomenon in Jamaican society – that of mother-son incest. (Illustration traced from child's drawings)

March 4, 2007), older data from the Child Guidance Clinic reported in an unpublished study commissioned by UNICEF in 1986, suggest that though there was a disproportionate number of female victims, male children at that time were also being seen. The Child Guidance Clinic has therefore been seeing this phenomenon for decades. In one case seen by the UWI Violence Prevention Programme in 2004 and referred by the Bureau of Women's Affairs, the feelings of the child, who was very articulate, are portrayed graphically in the illustration above.

Under-reporting of sexual crimes against women and girls – Solutions

The incidence of sexual crimes against women is admittedly under-reported in any society.

One response to this under-reporting of sexual violence against women is to employ female prosecuting law enforcement officials. Here, the findings of a research project done in the State of Illinois in the United States illustrated that the employment of female police officers was a mitigating force to reduce the stigma of sexual violence among women.[13] Female victims found it easier in that State to report incidents of sexual violence to female police officers rather than male police officers. Jamaican child welfare and law enforcement

---

13 *Time Magazine*, "Combating Violence in the Inner Cities of America," March 26, 2007.

authorities might take these factors into account in the development of procedures and policies for effective prosecution, if they are to effectively address the special problems of this population. In a recent commentary on this problem, medical practitioners and social workers from the Child Guidance Clinic (a special unit set up in the health care system for treating sexual abuse) expressed the concern that male children were in fact victims of adult females, many of whom were relatives, and other female associates well known to the children, such as household helpers (*Sunday Gleaner*, February 2010). Illustration 3 above shows a case of mother-son incest.

Sexual abuse – Community based extortion

It is possible that the phenomena described above are occurring as a result of changes at the community level in relation to values and norms associated with parenting, and specifically the extent to which children are seen as exploitable by sexual predators. Illustration 4 below by a 14-year-old girl clearly illustrates the dilemma that parents in the inner city find themselves in, when powerful criminals request sexual favours from their children in exchange for what are essentially social welfare benefits for their families, e.g. food, school books and loans for the maintenance of their households.

Illustration 4: A 14-year-old girl depicts the problem of criminal leaders who pressure parents to use their children as sexual pawns in exchange for material benefits needed for their family's survival. [Don: "Send your child tonight." Parent: "Why does it have to be me this time?"]

Use of technology in sexual abuse

Another issue that is illustrated by the various cases investigated and is captured in drawings of children, which so eloquently speak on behalf of themselves, is that of the use of technology (such as cell phones and Bluetooth) to record sexual abuse, and to transmit and replicate this material relatively easily in the form of DVDs and other electronic media, some of which have been made available commercially.[4] In Trinidad and Tobago there were isolated incidents of school boys using Bluetooth technology to disseminate sexual incidents concerning their female classmates. The policy response from the Ministry of Education in one Tobago school at the time was to ban cell phone use in the school system (Illustration 5).

Children as witnesses to sexual violence

In some situations which are not as common, children have been forced to witness sexual violence by dysfunctional parents, or by misguided community members to "toughen them up":

Illustration 5: An 11-year-old Jamaican school girl illustrates clearly the use of a weapon for coercion (on side table) and the use of a cell phone (above the bed) for disseminating the exploitation of children using new technologies

14   *Daily Gleaner*, 18 January 2003.

O N E 15-year-old male client from the UWI Violence Prevention Programme (UWIVPP) reported in 1996 that he was forced by a "self-acclaimed community leader" from his area to watch the gang rape of a 15-year-old girl by criminal adults in order to toughen him up. He states, "Miss, I pretend to act like it was nutten, but inside a mi miss, mi stomach sick." This child was taken to the UWIVPP by his grandmother in 1996 who was concerned about the role of this particular community leader in the socialization of her grandson.

Peer abuse - Cyber bullying linked to sexual violence

In other situations, children are victims and witnesses to sexual violence through the use of the new technology available through the taping of sexual acts by paedophiles using cell phones (Illustration 5) or to a lesser extent some children, mainly adolescents, are witnesses to pornographic material in selected forms of public transportation, mainly taxis with mobile DVD players and/or minibuses playing lewd songs and the showing of pornographic movies.

In some cases, other children may become indirectly involved in sexual violence when they are used by sexual predators to lure a child to the predator.

I N September 2004 a 38-year-old Jamaican woman who was a victim of sexual abuse as an adolescent over 20 years earlier, described this, while being treated at the UWIVPP, as the most traumatic aspect of her exploitative experience, as the sexual predator who abused her a second time was able to get to her by paying her schoolmate to take her unwittingly to him.

One disturbing case in Trinidad and Tobago which concerned child advocates and educators for months in 2005, was that of a 6-year-old boy who was raped by males who were both in the early stages of adolescence. The child was an unsuspecting victim, perhaps because the perpetrators were children themselves.

These cases highlight a dangerous trend in peer abuse which could be symptomatic of children accepting violence as a normal part of their lifestyle.

Human trafficking/prostitution

The issue of human trafficking as it relates to the exploitation of children puts them at risk for all forms of violence. This was first brought to the forefront of public consciousness in Jamaica when researchers began collecting and reporting formal data on child prostitution in Jamaica (Dunn 2002). In the report (which later led to the United States Government, "catching Jamaica with its pants down" in terms of its awareness of the internal trafficking of children for sexual services across parish boundaries), it was stated that there was at least one location in Jamaica where young girls willingly, for the most part, congregated to sell sexual and other questionable services to commercial brokers working on behalf of nightclubs and other businesses. It was disclosed that underage girls, many from the urban area and small towns of Jamaica, were prostituting themselves for money with or without the apparent consent of parents. Some parents reportedly encouraged the girls to use the money, in some cases, to fund their back-to-school expenses. This was happening at the same time that the Permanent Secretary in the Ministry of Social Security reported to Parliament that monies allocated to some social welfare services, particularly in the unit dealing with supplementary food distribution in that department, were largely underutilized. This situation resulted in the US Government lowering Jamaica's status regarding its (non-)adherence to treaties signed in relation to human trafficking. They held the Jamaican Government accountable for not prosecuting the adults responsible for the intra-island trafficking of adolescent girls despite the reported consensual nature of the girls' involvement. Though the figures did not show this activity as a massive problem in terms of the data, it seemed to be an extension of a pattern of non-convictions that mirrors the reporting of other generalized violence against children described later in this text as the "Ah Nuh Nutten" syndrome. Over the years, prior to the establishment of the Children's Registry in 2008, there had been an actual decrease in the reporting rates of sexual abuse.[14] Despite the Registry there have been few arrests and convictions of perpetrators,

---

14 Child Guidance Clinic Report, 2001.

though the figures showing the victims of rape are predominantly young children. This is of serious concern to social workers whose clients have to contend with being in the same community as their adult perpetrators.

Children as Victims of Kidnapping and Abduction
Jamaica/Trinidad and Tobago

Given the much bandied about theoretical position that suggests that crime and violence are fuelled by inequity, and that crime is closely linked to economic problems associated with unemployment and underemployment (Levy 1996) one wonders why the rate of this kind of crime and violence is increasing so rapidly in Trinidad and Tobago, given the comparatively healthier state of its economy vis-à-vis Jamaica. This suggests that like so many other social problems, crime and violence in the Caribbean are fuelled by factors other than those put forward by the traditional social and economic theories, and must be analysed differentially according to territory, if the problem is to be managed effectively across the Caribbean.

The pattern of the abduction and kidnapping of children in Trinidad is a little different from that in Jamaica, as the abductions there are closely linked to reprisals as a result of the drug trade. In the Jamaican situation, children from the working class who are abducted are often sexually assaulted and then killed, presumably to protect the identity of the perpetrator. Children from middle-class families are kidnapped for ransom, but these cases are few and far between. Kidnappings in Trinidad are much more common, but there are fewer murders of children and there are less instances of rape of these abducted children. In the Jamaican context, gang reprisals are often associated with these abductions and children are involved as victims, as a means to "send a message" to an adult member of the child's family. In other cases of missing children in Jamaica, anecdotal reports suggest that the children are runaways from abusive or other difficult situations. It is important to note, therefore, that in cases of Trinidad and Tobago, kidnappings of children are more commonplace, while in Jamaica abductions and runaway behaviour are the main reasons for missing children (Illustration 6).

Illustration 6: Child's drawing depicting a kidnapping, Trinidad and Tobago

High technology alert systems – cooperation needed from public

The abduction and kidnapping of children by criminals who seek to receive monetary compensation from relatives and other family members as ransom is a relatively new phenomenon in the Caribbean. As discussed above, some of these children are eventually murdered, while others, particularly in Jamaica, have remained on the police records as missing for years. In 2005 the number of missing children in Jamaica reached an all-time high where the Constabulary Communication Network (CCN) reported more than 100 children missing over a two-year period, the majority of them being girls. Girls are therefore most at risk for abductions in Jamaica because, as mentioned earlier, most of these victims are raped and then murdered. There is a tremendous need for private non-government organizations (NGOs) and advocacy groups, as well as state agencies in Jamaica and Trinidad and Tobago to address the problem of missing children with some urgency, using massive public advertising, including billboards, as well as high-tech tracking systems and alert systems (e.g. Ananda Alert in Jamaica) to find these children. The lack of attention to this very serious problem has resulted in a sense of complacency in the criminal world which allows them to continue to see children and adolescents as easy and soft targets for their criminal pursuits. Prevention programmes to alert children and parents in the school system must address this issue aggressively so that all children, including those in early childhood, are prepared to deal with the threat of abductions and kidnappings as they journey to and from school.

Other forms of violence affecting children in other Caribbean territories

Other types of situations documented by police blotters where children in Jamaica are victims often resulting in violent death included suicide, drowning, electrocution, and fire. The data on attempted suicide indicate that there were 46 cases of adolescents (10 to 19 year-olds) who presented in Jamaica in 2001 at public hospitals for intervention. It is worthy of note that female adolescents were eleven times more likely to have attempted suicide than males in 2001. Another unique difference between Trinidad and Tobago and Jamaica is that there is an inordinately high rate of suicide in young girls and women aged 15 to 24 in Trinidad and Tobago. Though this phenomenon is reportedly linked to ethnicity occurring predominantly in the Indian population, the figures are significant enough for social policies to be put in place to prevent this very serious problem.

In Trinidad and Tobago, there has also been a phenomenal increase in the serious crime of abduction and kidnapping of children and business owners. Trinidad has also seen a massive increase in the homicidal rate from 78 murders in the January to March period in 2000, as against 170 for the same period in 2006.[15] Child murder is also of concern, as shown in Figure 13.

Summary

It is apparent from the above discussion that children who are victims of violence become victims as a result of a variety of factors. It has become apparent that the data relating to (i) the murder of children (the most extreme form of violence against children), (ii) sexual violence, as well as (iii) the kidnapping of children, seem to be part of a general pattern of violence which affects children in their homes, schools and communities.

Though one must acknowledge that Jamaica has always diverged from the rest of the Commonwealth Caribbean in having a much higher level of violent crime, and greater severity in the nature of

---

15   *Trinidad Guardian*, 1 March 2006

Figure 13: *Deaths by age – Trinidad and Tobago 1998*

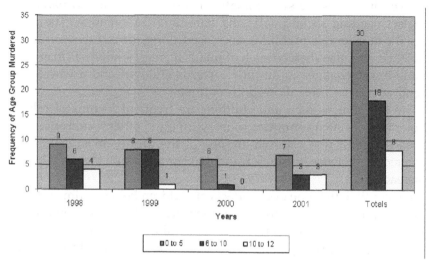

Source: Statistical Office, Trinidad and Tobago

the crimes in relation to that of its Caribbean neighbours, Trinidad and Tobago is also showing new patterns in terms of terrorist crime (as evidenced by small scale public bombings, and the increasing incidence of kidnapping of children and adults, which were heretofore relatively uncommon patterns of crime in that Caribbean territory).

Need for collection and documentation of child mortality data

Close monitoring of child mortality data as shown above could assist in macro level planning so that policies can be put into place to prevent these deaths. For example, data on traffic accidents suggest that in 2001 the deaths of children by traffic accidents decreased dramatically in May and June when compared to other months of the year. This could possibly be linked to children being off the roads during the summer holidays. An awareness of this kind of information by policy makers perhaps through research-based websites (see http://ccwrn.org) could result in policy makers in the child welfare arena being able to plan ahead to avoid child mortality in that area.

It is to be noted from the discussion in this chapter that all categories of violent death, such as drowning, death by fire, as well as childhood murders increased over the three-year period 1998-2001. Recent data show a continuing trend up to 2008.[16] The causes of death which showed increases are symptomatic of serious societal and parental neglect needing social policy and parenting intervention. The fact that the murder rate of children increased alongside all other forms of violence, and also showed such dramatic increases, suggests massive value-based changes in attitude towards children and a worrying trend which has been allowed to continue.

The fact that women and children are frequent victims of other violent crimes such as murder, robbery, rape and other sexual offences would suggest that children are one of the groups most seriously affected by violence in Jamaica, and that the impact on them has been far-reaching.

It is possible that one of the effects of children being victims is that they may become perpetrators as they grow older. The other side of violence in Jamaica, therefore, is that children are perpetrators as well as victims. This phenomenon will be investigated in the next chapter.

---

16 CCN, Incidence of Children Killed in Jamaica 2005-2008.

CHAPTER TWO

CHILDREN AS PERPETRATORS
The Other Side of Violence

P A T T E R N S of youth violence globally point to the presence of youth who increasingly are not victims but perpetrators. When one looks at the data in Jamaica which refer to persons arrested for major crimes such as murder, shooting, robbery, breaking and entering, rape and carnal abuse in 2005, of a total of 824 incidents, 10% involved children between the ages of 12 to 15 years. Of the 824 cases, 90% or 736 involved children and young people in the age range 16 to 20 years as perpetrators.

Like the rest of the world, therefore, when one examines the pattern of these crimes, the young adult group is most involved in the criminal activities and violence generally. In Jamaica, young people continue to be both the victims of violence and the group that contributes to violence. The number of youths arrested, jailed or murdered in Jamaica in 2003 was twice the rate of the general population.[18] In examining the percentage of crimes committed by youths, 83% of all murders were committed by youths aged 20 years and under, 72% of youths were responsible for all shootings, 98% for sexual crimes (rape and carnal abuse) and 27% for breaking and entering (UNICEF 2006). This suggests that between early and late adolescence there is an urgent need for violence prevention and other support services for these age cohorts.[19]

---

18 Human Development Report: socioeconomic policy framework (2006).
19 UN Secretary General's report on violence against children – Regional Office for Latin America & the Caribbean.

This is reinforced by the fact that 19% of the total number of violence related injuries reported to public hospitals in Jamaica were committed by individuals under 17 years (Ward et al. 2001). This supports the fact that there is some involvement of children and youth as perpetrators in the present scourge of violence being experienced in Jamaica.

The fact is that when one looks at the data historically, there is evidence that this pattern has been in place for at least a decade. In 2001, 253 young adults in the age range 16 to 20 were arrested for serious crimes. Of that number, 72 (28.5%) committed murder, while 83 (32.8%) were arrested for shooting. The greatest number of these youths (98 or 38.7%) were arrested for rape and carnal abuse (see Figure 14, page 54).[20] This suggests that the nature of youth crime and violence is such that those who are perpetrators (most of them male) are involved in serious and violent crimes as they approach the end of adolescence. It also suggests that intervention must take place earlier to prevent this spike in the rates of serious crimes in this age group.

Boys at Risk For Violence

The issue of boys being at risk is supported by data from the Department of Correctional Services which suggest that most crimes perpetrated by children are, in fact, committed by boys. This is reportedly due to the fact that among boys school drop-outs level is high, and more exposure to violence.[21] This is due to the differing patterns of socialization between the genders where girls in the Caribbean are reportedly more sheltered by parents and by members of their communities, including the police.[22] This correlates to the well documented Caribbean phrase, and is a well established parenting practise: "loose the bull, tie the heifer". [23]

Another feature worthy of note regarding male child perpetrators is the fact that there is also a disproportionate representation of males in correctional institutions. Of a total of 235 children detained in 2006, 183 or 77% of them were boys.[24] The primary reasons for admission

---

20 Planning Institute of Jamaica, *The Jamaican Child* (PIOJ, 2004).

21 UNICEF, Situation Analysis on Gender Disparities in Jamaica (update/2007)

22 Focus Group discussion between community social workers and members of the Jamaica Constabulary Force, Maxfield Park Division.

23 Brown et al. (1993).

24 Department of Correctional Services, Ministry of Security & Justice (2007).

to the correctional institutions were (a) breaking and entering, and stealing (12%); (b) wounding (12%); (c) use of dangerous drugs (11%); (d) uncontrollable behaviour (9%). During the same period, 21% of girls were admitted for care and protection, 17% for uncontrollable behaviour and 4% for wounding. One interesting finding reported by the Department of Correctional Services in 2008 is that in recent years more girls are being arrested for possession of weapons, as criminals target them as couriers to transport guns, sometimes in their school bags.

Early Detection, Assessment and Intervention Within Schools

The above data suggest that within the school system there is need for early detection and intervention for boys in particular, who are at risk for conduct disorder and other behavioural problems which can lead to violent crime. For girls there is an urgent need for assessment and intervention to deal with emotional problems arising out of issues such as sexual abuse. There is therefore the need for preventive programmes such as after-school and other community-based activi-

Photo 4: Tredegar Park children attending a GSAT stress buster activity organized by the UWIVPP and the Peace Management Initiative. Student Tereseta Charles from St. Vincent and June Scott, clinical social work graduate, helped to facilitate group activities

ties to target boys in latency age and early adolescence for violence prevention and conflict resolution programmes. It is also important to involve them in activities such as sport, music, the visual and other fine arts, as well as technical skills that can engage their creative energies long before they get to middle adolescence.

Children as Perpetrators (All Forms of Violence)

Table 3: *Children as perpetrators of all forms of violence*

Level of Involvement	Description of Circumstance
Directly Involved	Perpetrators of physical violence, e.g., as bullies (older children acting as extortionists in school, cyber bullies*), perpetrators of sexual violence (peer abuse) *children who use text messaging or Internet to bully peers
Children at Risk	Children who are in difficult circumstances – namely children with emotional and behavioural problems which remain undetected and untreated in the school system, Children for whom there are no intervention services unless they commit a crime, Children in alternative parenting environments, such as Children's Homes / Group Homes, Correctional facilities, children whose parent(s) have migrated, died or are incarcerated, and children with inadequate parental supervision, e.g. street and working children
Indirectly Involved	Children who witness and encourage other children to perpetuate physical violence (e.g. bullies, cliques/supporters), children who witness sexual violence perpetrated on a child as part of a gang of other children, children at risk. i.e. children in groups or children's homes who learn violent behaviour from association with peers, or who are reacting to ill treatment by rebellion and aggression

As shown in the above discussion and summarized in the chart above, children who are perpetrators include children who are bullies, those who assault others and show disrespect to authority figures, and children involved in extortion from weaker and/or younger children in their schools and communities. It is to be noted, however, that some of the factors which predispose these children to violence may be rooted in the nature of parenting that the children receive. These and other factors will be discussed in the chapter that follows.

Nature of crimes perpetrated by children – prevalence

As discussed previously, in 2001, "*A total of 72 murders, 83 shootings and 98 acts of rape and carnal abuse, were attributed to children in 2001.*"[25]

In order to put this data in perspective, it is important to note that of all major crimes reported in 2001, 6% were committed by children under 17 years of age, and as a percentage of all violent crimes 19%, as shown in Figure 15, were committed by children and youths between the ages of 13 and 19 years. As discussed earlier therefore, it is important to note that the 2005 data illustrate the fact that there is a major increase in prevalence rates, once male child perpetrators get to 16 years old.

Illustration 7: This picture was drawn by a 10-year-old perpetrator of bullying

---

25 Planning Institute of Jamaica, *The Jamaican Child*, op. cit., 2004.

Figure 14: *Children as perpetrators of violence in 2001*

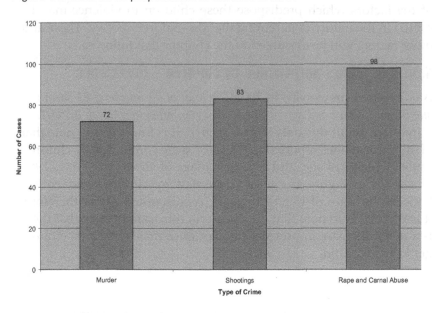

Figure 15: *Percentage of children as perpetrators of violence*

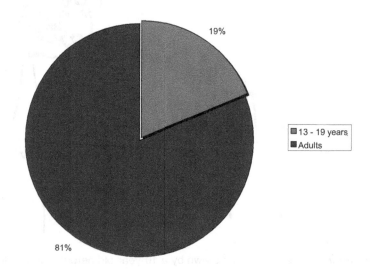

Rural/urban differentials

In terms of rural/urban differentials, the majority of perpetrators of major crimes were again in the urban centres. Over 70.0% of the murders committed by children occurred in Kingston, St. Andrew and St. Catherine combined.[26] The same is true for shootings. An important point to note is that perpetrators of serious crimes often exhibit violent behaviours during school age whether they are in rural or urban schools. It is therefore important for the Ministry of Education to put in place well developed violence prevention programmes, as mentioned earlier, for early identification, detection and treatment which can be accessed across the country in both rural and urban centres.

Peer to peer sexual violence

One interesting phenomenon which comes from the anecdotal reports of teachers, guidance counsellors and caregivers at private and state run Child Care institutions in the last five years, is the existence of peer sexual abuse. This involves the rape and sexual exploitation of young girls and adolescents by young adolescent males and females individually and in groups. Individual and group incidents were mainly reported from children's homes (Tomlinson 2010).

This could be explained by the socialization experiences of youngsters who have grown up in a culture where sexual abuse is seen as "normal" and where abusers go unpunished (Crawford-Brown 2000). Another explanation offered by the results of one adolescent research project in Jamaica found that at an early age boys are taught that sex brings pleasure and social status, whereas girls learn that sexual activity is something secret and shameful.[27] As a result, sexual abuse is not reported to the authorities by victims or their parents and the problem continues unabated (Gayle 2004).

In order to look comprehensively at the problem of children as perpetrators it is important to also look at the general causative factors that have been documented in the literature for behavioural problems related to conduct disorder, a disorder considered to be a precursor for criminal behaviour in adulthood.

---

26 Police Metro Division.
27 UNICEF Situation Analysis and Gender Disparities in Jamaica – update 2007.

Major theoretical perspectives on the aetiology of violence

Numerous studies have been conducted to examine the development of conduct disorder and the emergence of violent behaviour in children and adolescents. Some studies are focused on the relationship between violent behaviour in childhood and the later development of criminal behaviour. In one study, the definition of conduct disorder as that of a pathological state within which delinquent acts take place (McMahon & Wells 1991) is used. Many of these studies look at aetiological factors relating to delinquency and conduct disorder (Schior 1983; Orcutt 1987), while others have been largely descriptive of the nature of these disorders (McMahon & Wells 1991). Other studies have attempted to investigate associations between delinquency and a wide variety of variables which include social variables such as family relationships (Rutter 1972; Khron & Massey 1980), peer group influences (Hoghughi 1988), as well as biological (Lewis 1985) and other sociological variables (Cloward & Ohlin 1960; Bandura 1973; Akers 1964). The different theoretical approaches will now be presented. If one summarizes the historical roots of the aetiology of conduct disorder, one finds that the theorists tend to discuss the phenomenon from three major perspectives. These can be described as psychological, biological and sociological.

Psychological perspectives

The psychological basis of violence involving youth may be described as being represented by two major schools of thought in the literature: the Psychoanalytic School, which represents those theories that offer psycho-dynamic explanations for conduct disorders; and the Behavioural School, which represents two classes of theories, namely, character disorder and learned family characteristics. Character disorder theories are those that see conduct disorder as being part of a personality or character disorder acquired through learned behaviour, e.g. the Temperament Theory. Theories which reflect the notion of learned family characteristics are those that see conduct disorder as a result of faulty child rearing practices influenced by numerous family characteristics and variables, and from which the child learns faulty patterns of behaviour, e.g. the Social Learning Theory and Attachment Theory (Kernberg & Chazzan 1991).

Sociological perspectives

The sociological viewpoint emphasizes the importance of the social environment as a causative factor, particularly in aggressive and violent behaviour. The major contribution of the sociological theories, therefore, is that they transcend the natural limitations of the biological and psychological explanations and point to the social complexity of delinquency. The landmark Shaw and McKay study (1931) showed that communities with high delinquency rates were characterized by poverty, economic deprivation, and physical deterioration. The geographical areas investigated were high crime inner-city neighbourhoods populated by recent arrivals in the mass migration to the United States in the 1930s. These areas, the researchers found, had a high population of foreign-born and Black residents who were often geographically very mobile and transient. Shaw and McKay described these conditions as conducive to antisocial behaviour. They argued that a continuation of poverty as well as poor living conditions aroused frustrations and discontent in such families which in turn fostered a hostile attitude to society. They also expressed the view that conflicting cultural standards and rapidly changing population made it difficult for the parents studied to parent efficiently. They found that children, particularly boys, had many aggressive antisocial models in many families; the boys' fathers provided such models. Bearing in mind the historical context of the study, these results were not surprising.

Demographic characteristics

A few researchers have looked at the issue of demographic characteristics such as the socioeconomic status of the families to determine an association between this variable and the incidence of violent behaviours. Triton and Steward (1982) point to the absence of a positive association between the presence of conduct disorder and socioeconomic status. One other related study which supports this finding was conducted by D'Alberquerque (1984) who investigated adult crime rates in relation to socioeconomic status in the Caribbean. That researcher found that the two variables – socioeconomic factors and violent behaviour – were not associated.

The behavioural school - learned family characteristics

Though dated, the primary contributors to the body of knowledge surrounding learned aggressive responses and its relationship to personality development and, consequently, personality disorders which result in violent behaviour such as conduct disorders and antisocial personality disorders were Bandura and Walters (1973), and Klieg and Bandura (1973). The research in this period proliferated between the late 1950s and early 1970s. These works were preceded by G.V. Hamilton (1923) and an unnamed group of Yale researchers around 1933, who found that in a group of 300 conduct-disordered children, over 70% had histories of aggressive personality since early childhood. These investigators, particularly Bandura and his colleagues, sought to establish the fact that child rearing had an influence on the development of aggressive personality in these children.

These research findings raised the question of whether there is some degree of modelling of parental behaviour in terms of the tendency for children to imitate behaviours they have witnessed or experienced, as occurs with imitation of criminal behaviour, or when there is parental psychopathology. In both cases, Lewis (1985) suggests that there might be "identification with the aggressor" (p.141) which she describes as "a behavioural manifestation of a child having grown up in an atmosphere of violence" as occurs when there is chronic physical abuse of children.

Another theoretical perspective which relates to learned behaviour is that of the Attachment Theory, where it is assumed that conduct-disordered children share a feeling of being unloved and uncared-for, and their world is constructed around feelings of rejection and abandonment (Kernberg & Chazzan 1991). The Attachment Theory draws on the concept of the Objects Relations Theory, as well as a concept related to the development and dynamic interaction of the psyche. As a result of continued interactions with the world of objects and individuals, the child constructs models of the world and the people within it (Bowlby 1969/1973/1980; Brotherton 1985). The presence of violent behaviour patterns in children, it is assumed, therefore represents long-term difficulties in terms of relations with significant persons in their lives.

Social learning theories

For over three decades, Social Learning Theory has been used to explain the evaluation, treatment, and causation of violent behaviour

among youth within the context of the family (particularly in relation to the modelling of parental behaviour (Bandura & Walters 1959;
Gardener 1974). One useful theoretical model based on the Social
Learning Theory suggests that the learning of deviant behaviour is a
complex interaction of important learning dimensions in the child's
environment, namely, parent/child interaction in the family, teacher/
child interaction in the context of the school, and peer interaction in
the social environment (Stuart, Jayaratne, & Tripodi 1976). According
to this model, pro-social responses are discarded or neglected, and
negative behaviours are reinforced over time by peers in the social
environment, thus resulting in deviant behaviour which may include
criminal and violent activities. Later, theoretical models such as
that of Elliot, Huizinga, and Ageton (1985) point to the role of prior
delinquent behaviour in the eventual development of more serious
criminal behaviour. Yet other theorists in the past two decades have
emphasized the importance of parental modelling and family stabil-
ity as deterrents to delinquent, and possibly, criminal behaviours
(Khron & Massey 1980). Much of the more recent research has not
changed these basic findings.

Understanding the Development of Violent Behaviour in Children and Adolescence

Essentials of a new theoretical learning model

Based on the above discussion, the writer developed an integrated
model summarizing the most useful ideas from previous models. This
model, originally developed by Jayaratne and Tripodi and adapted
by the author, suggests that criminal behaviour develops gradually
from childhood, operating in four major learning dimensions These
dimensions are as follows: (1) A Psycho-Biological Dimension which
refers to the existence of personality traits and cognitive abilities; (2)
A Societal Dimension which refers to the involvement of the agencies of socialization such as the family and the school; (3) A Social
Dimension which refers to the degree to which the behaviour is
reinforced negatively or positively by the different systems developed by the society to deal with the offender or perpetrator; and (4)
A Psychological Dimension where the violent or criminal behaviour
may become internalized or discarded. As a result of the latter dimension, deviant behaviour may persist or may be re-directed into other
non-criminal channels.

Chart 2: *Multi-dimensional Model – development of deviant behaviour*

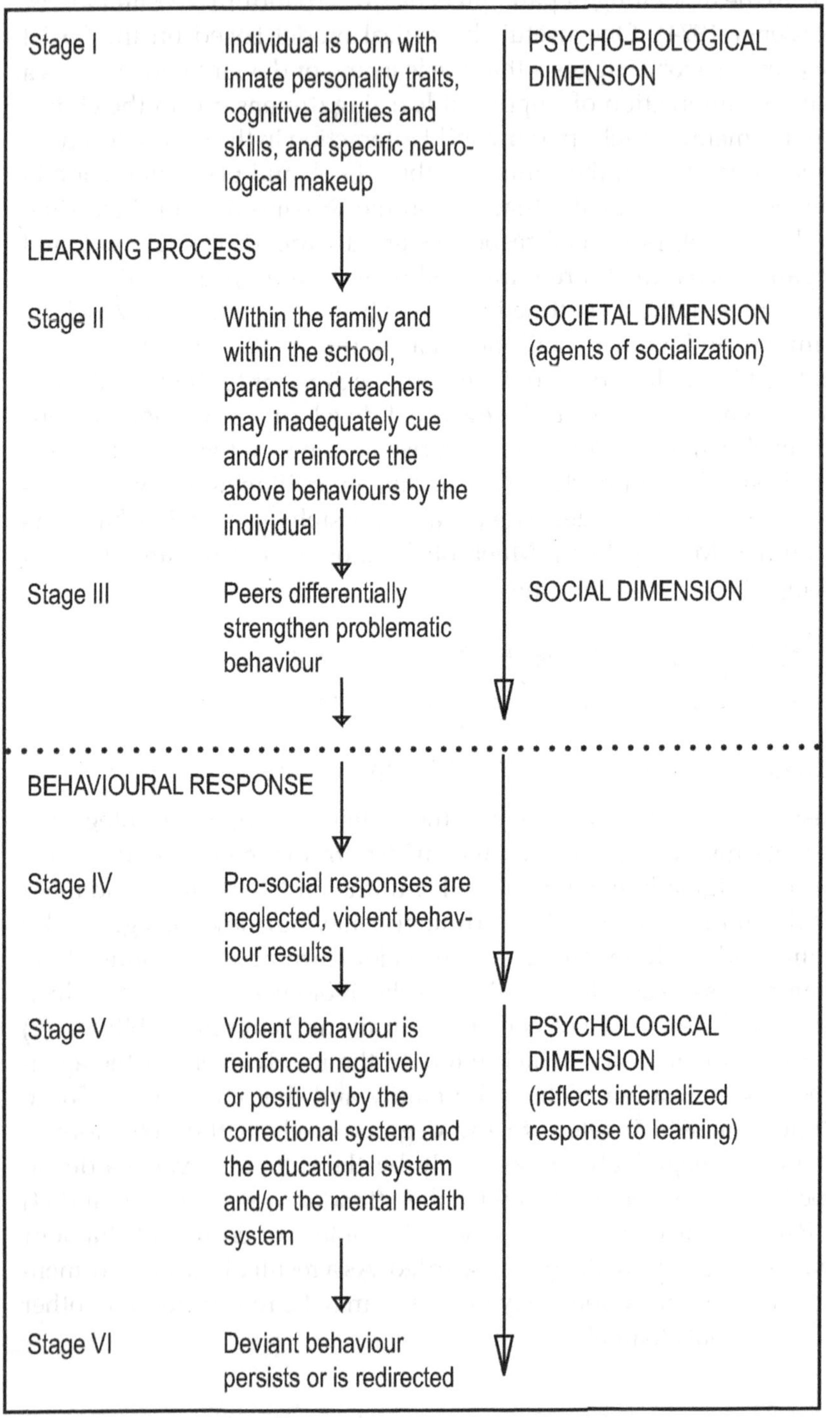

Stage I	Individual is born with innate personality traits, cognitive abilities and skills, and specific neurological makeup	PSYCHO-BIOLOGICAL DIMENSION
LEARNING PROCESS	↓	
Stage II	Within the family and within the school, parents and teachers may inadequately cue and/or reinforce the above behaviours by the individual ↓	SOCIETAL DIMENSION (agents of socialization)
Stage III	Peers differentially strengthen problematic behaviour ↓	SOCIAL DIMENSION ▽
BEHAVIOURAL RESPONSE	↓	
Stage IV	Pro-social responses are neglected, violent behaviour results ↓	▽
Stage V	Violent behaviour is reinforced negatively or positively by the correctional system and the educational system and/or the mental health system ↓	PSYCHOLOGICAL DIMENSION (reflects internalized response to learning)
Stage VI	Deviant behaviour persists or is redirected	▽

Development of deviant behaviour via a "multi-dimensional model"

As shown in the model (Chart 2), the various dimensions explain the cumulative development of violent behaviour as the child is socialized.

The **Psycho-biological Dimension** assumes that at the first stage of the child's development the individual is born with and possesses innate personality traits, cognitive abilities and skills, and a specific neurological make-up which may or may not predispose him/her to violent behaviour.

The **Societal Dimension** refers to the second stage of the learning process which takes place within the family and within the school. At this point parents and teachers may inadequately cue and/or reinforce the above-mentioned behaviours by the individual.

Social Dimension. At the third stage the learning process continues and this is where peers and significant others differentially strengthen problematic behaviour. This is where the child may begin to develop relationships with peers who are negative role models (gangs or other socially unacceptable groups), that is, pro-social or antisocial.

It is important to note that the individual may show a behavioural response to what is occurring in the learning process and thus the child moves into Stage IV where pro-social responses are neglected and violent behaviour may result.

The **Psychological Dimension.** It is presumed that at this stage violent behaviour is reinforced negatively or positively by the correctional system and the educational system as well as the mental health system. This suggests that the effectiveness of these systems will determine whether the child becomes violent in adulthood as their responses will re-direct or direct the individual to a behavioural reaction.

Violent behaviour not 'caught' in childhood

This writer suggests that a breakdown in the social service delivery system in Jamaica is an important component which does not "catch" violent behaviour when it can be redirected. Thus, a disproportionate number of our children in difficult circumstances end up as perpetrators.

In keeping with the developmental model of antisocial behaviour outlined by Patterson et al. (1989), which suggests that a combination of factors throughout the child's development includes ineffective parenting as one of the variables that affect the development of violent and antisocial behaviour in the child. This text posits however, that it is the responsibility of the various components of the social service systems within the state apparatus to redirect violent behaviour when it presents itself, wherever possible.

Why do Some Children Become Criminals?

Children in difficult circumstances

One of the questions that concerns social planners and social prac-titioners globally is what proportion of adolescents in the society are perpetrators of violent crimes, and how do these perpetrators become criminals in the first place. In the Caribbean, this is also a matter of some concern as early intervention in the lives of children and adolescents before they become adult criminals is a strategy that could save scarce resources that would be otherwise used for law enforcement and crime fighting at a later stage. The question that must be answered, therefore, is: What are the factors which fuel violence among youth and what are the factors which make some children become criminals, and not others?

The previous discussion outlined a conceptual framework for understanding how violent behaviour develops in children. Another important set of issues that affects the development of this behaviour in children, however, is the extent to which the child is at risk for violence, as a result of being in special or difficult circumstances. In Jamaica, there are a range of difficult circumstances that children experience which put them at risk for exhibiting violence. These circumstances are discussed in detail below and illustrated in Chart 3.

There are a wide range of circumstances and specific situations which seem to make children more susceptible to the different acts of violence at the level of the individual child and the family. Those children who are more prone to become victims as well as perpetrators of violence include children living and working on the streets as well as those in children's homes and correctional facilities, those children who are unsupervised and neglected for prolonged periods due to absent parents, children who are abused, children of parents who are incarcerated or who have migrated (internally or externally) as well as those children whose parents have died. Individual and family factors affecting children who are predisposed to violence as perpetrators include all of the factors identified for children who are

Chart 3: *Model showing children in difficult circumstances*

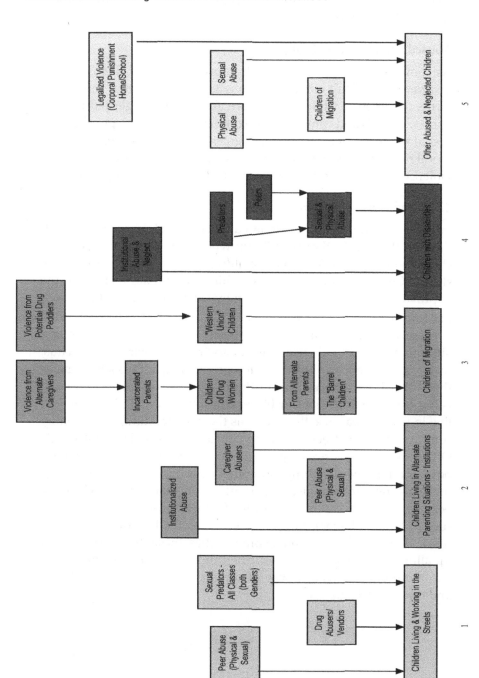

victims, but in addition it is important to note that many of these children need alternative parenting arrangements.

Abused and Neglected Children

As shown in Chart 3, many children in Jamaica find themselves in a variety of difficult circumstances which place them at risk for all forms of violence. Children who are abused and neglected in their homes, schools and communities experience emotional, physical and sexual abuse, as well as varying degrees of medical, educational and moral neglect. These circumstances place them at risk for all forms of violence and abuse from their parents, older relatives or peers.

Street and working children

Street and working children in Jamaica can be categorised as (i) children **on** the streets, that is, children who work on the streets; or (ii) children **of** the streets, who are children who live **and** work on the streets. Children on the streets are children who are there with the approval of their parents so they can live at home and use their work to contribute to the household income (Crawford-Brown 1996).

These children are also at risk from drug dealers, addicts and abusers, who routinely use violence to "peddle their wares". Thus, their very presence as witnesses to various illegal transactions place them at risk and place them in the middle of retaliatory battles. It is important to note that Caribbean children, particularly those who live in urban areas, use the streets as their playground, and in many communities the streets could be considered as their "front yard". Often, middle class sexual predators offer the children, particularly boys, food, money, clothing, and other basic necessities in exchange for sexual favours. It is also important to note that children who have been sexually abused are at risk for further abuse because they are seen as being "damaged goods" and, given the lack of intervention services in schools and in their communities, these children often end up allowing themselves to be further abused. Sometimes they even become promiscuous as a way of coping with their sense of shame and low self-esteem.

Children who are disabled

Illustration 8: Drawing by a deaf-mute girl

Children who are disabled/physically or mentally challenged, are particularly at risk in Jamaican society because, like all persons with disabilities, they are stigmatized and discriminated against. In addition, they are considered soft targets for sexual abuse because they are often less able to communicate what is happening to them. Illustration 8 is a drawing done by a 6-year-old deaf-mute girl who was suspected of being sexually abused. This is the diagram she drew when, with the assistance of a signer, she was asked to depict what had happened to her. With effective intervention and therapy using the services of a counsellor who knew sign language, she was helped to ventilate and talk and to communicate with her caregiver about the abuse.

Children in alternate living situations

These groups of children are those in children's homes and in foster care and they are particularly at risk for a range of violent experiences because the agencies given the responsibility to care for them are ill-equipped in terms of human and material resources to do so. Most of these children have serious emotional problems as a result of years of undue neglect, as well as issues of attachment and loss which had never been dealt with therapeutically. The children's homes and foster homes in which they reside are merely custodial, and for decades have been criticized as breeding grounds for dysfunction. Many of these institutions act as a revolving door which the children go through and then produce another generation of children who need to be institutionalized for the same kinds of emotional and behavioural problems with which their parents were afflicted (Crawford-Brown 1999). Within these institutions sometimes there may be cases of institutional abuse as a result of difficulties such as overcrowding and the lack of therapeutic services and adequately trained caregivers in these institutions. Due to these factors, peer abuse within these institutions also places some children at risk for interpersonal violence such as bullying and sometimes peer-based sexual abuse (Crawford-Brown 1993), as mentioned above.

Children of migration

The issue of the impact of migration on children in the Caribbean has not received very much mention in the literature on violence affecting children. There is little empirical data which suggest that some of the children left behind in the Caribbean by the migration of their parents are at risk for exhibiting behavioural problems which may manifest as adult violent behaviour. In an unpublished study done at the Mico Youth Counselling and Development Centre in 1992, it was determined that in a sample of 140 who presented with behavioural problems, 60% had experienced the absence of one or more parent due to migration (Crawford-Brown 1992).

There are also problems associated with children of migration in Jamaica which places them at risk for violence. The children of migration who are at risk for violence in its various forms could be described as exhibiting the following characteristics:

The "Barrel Children" phenomenon. This is a term coined by Jamaican social work practitioners which refers to

> those children who have been left behind as a result of external migration and who are often the victims of ineffective alternative parenting arrangements. These children receive material gifts in corrugated barrels but may lack the emotional nurturance that they so desperately need (Crawford-Brown 1999; Crawford-Brown & Rattray 2001).

Other more contemporary migration related issues affecting children include the phenomenon of what is referred to as **"Western Union Children"**. This is another phrase which has become part of the "social vernacular" of Jamaican service providers where, as a result of the migration process, children are sent regular remittances from overseas through local money transfer agencies, but the parents themselves through the direct control of money, which can then be used at the discretion of the child. There is often little adult supervision, and parenting is done by "remote control" through the readily available cellular phone and other communication technology – parents checking on their children sometimes once per week (Crawford-Brown 2006).

There are a number of other issues which predispose children and young adolescents to violence, which are related to migration. These include:

"Children of Drug Courier Moms". This is another term coined by social practitioners, which refers to children left behind by mothers, and more recently fathers, who have been incarcerated by law enforcement systems overseas as a result of their involvement in drug trafficking. These children are sometimes abandoned suddenly and are left without parents for long unplanned periods due to the nature of their parent's offense which often takes place during overseas travel.

Other children of migration are children who are part of a return migration process as a result of deportation of parents. These latter issues are often directly linked to criminal activities and so are discussed in more detail below.

Returning residents/deportee issues

There are also other related new problems such as the issue of the return migration of children and adults, where some of the adult returning residents who have criminal records, are emerging as community leaders, notwithstanding the fact that they have a history of criminal behaviour in the societies from which some may have been deported.

Of particular concern is the emergence of a pattern of social behaviour where these returning residents who are deported become informal community leaders or "dons" as they are referred to locally. They provide social welfare services for children and families of community members in the form of school fees for children, books, clothing and food (see Illustration 027, chapter four). This behaviour has over time begun to affect the nature of the socialization of young children through the establishment of new community standards and norms regarding the physical and sexual abuse and discipline of children and child rearing, as sexual abuse of the children of recipients of these social welfare "benefits" is considered "payment for services offered".

In addition, these self-appointed "community leaders" provide what one mother described as "work" and "skills training" for adolescents through gangs and involvement in "illicit activities" such as drug courier services. Despite the illegal nature of these activities, they are seen as positive benefits by families because the community leaders also provide opportunities for migration for the women and men involved, and employment takes place through the criminalized international networks within and outside of the Caribbean.

Return migration of children

Children are also sometimes informally "deported" by their families from metropolitan countries to the Caribbean. Wint (1986) reported that in case studies of 30 children returned to Jamaica in 1986, a significant proportion of them were sent back to their country for being "rude". When probed, respondents included issues such as reporting of sexual abuse to authorities in the host country. In 2002, the Jamaican Child Development Agency which has international responsibilities for receiving deported children and seeing to their welfare, reported that 33 Jamaican children were deported from the USA, Canada and Britain. Recent reports from that agency suggest that many such cases are due to fraudulent documentation of children travelling alone, or children whose parents are involved in illicit activities. However, there have been isolated cases of children being used by adult parents to export drugs, i.e. hidden in clothing or on their person (*Daily Gleaner* 2002).

This again points to a breakdown in the ethics of parents and the values of our families. The placing of such large numbers of children at risk in this way is a new phenomenon in Caribbean society and suggests that parents will take risks regardless of the consequences. This is not just desperate and foolhardy but speaks to moral neglect of our children. The result is that the children's experience at the beginning can be devastating as a result of the lack of trust generated between parents and children, as well as the dislocation and instability of being moved back and forth internationally, which in turn affect their emotional and psychological well-being.

Women as drug couriers and the impact on t he children left behind

The impact of the drug trade is a serious challenge as the Caribbean grapples with the reality that its geography places it in the unenviable position of being a convenient transshipment port for drug traffickers across the Western hemisphere.

As mentioned earlier, one of the ways that this has affected contemporary Caribbean society is through the use of women as drug couriers. Again much of this trafficking is controlled by criminals at the local community level. When these women are caught by law enforcement officials overseas, this again has serious implications for the well-being of the children left behind in the Caribbean as these children are left unsupervised or in inadequate alternative parenting arrangements. Again the issue of the choices being made by these parents raises questions about the ethics and values associated with parenting and whether ethics and values are in fact changing in different ways across the different classes in society as individual families grapple with the challenges of harsh economic realities. The extent to which these issues contribute to deviant behaviour in these children left behind is an issue that is of concern. This will be discussed in more detail in the next chapter on parenting.

Given the special circumstances discussed above, namely children of migration; children in abused and neglected situations; children living and working on the streets; children with physical, mental and other challenges; as well as children in alternate parenting situations, it is important to note that though these situations are difficult, only some of these children and adolescents will exhibit violent behaviour and commit criminal acts. The question that still needs to be answered therefore is: Given the general reality of poverty that places children at risk and puts them in difficult circumstances, what causes some of the children in these situations to become model citizens while others become criminals?

Why Do Children Become Criminals?

Caribbean research

The author sought to investigate and test the causative model of violent behaviour (Jayaratne & Tripodi 1976) with a Caribbean population of adolescents. The purpose of such an aetiological framework was to better understand the development of conduct disorder and violent behaviour in children and adolescents, as well as to determine what broad factors were found to be most associated with violent behaviour. The methodology involved comparing two groups of children and adolescents to determine the degree of association between the presence of conduct disorder and (i) structural and functional family factors, (ii) peer group factors, and (iii) neuro-biological factors. The study group consisted of 70 boys who were deemed to be conduct disordered based on DSM IV criteria (Diagnostic Statistical manual of Mental Disorders) and the second group consisted of 70 children and adolescent boys who did not present with behavioural problems. Both groups were matched for socioeconomic status and intellectual capacity.

Empirical factors associated with the development of violent behaviour

Based on the research findings conducted by the author in 1993 and 2004, thirteen variables were identified as being associated with violent behaviour (see Appendix IV). Other Caribbean researchers have isolated factors associated with aggression in children as being related to exposure to violence and family conflict (Meeks-Gardener 2006), as well as exposure to corporal punishment through the school system (Samms-Vaughan 2004). Of the thirteen variables identified in this study, the author sought to isolate those which appeared to interface. Using cluster analysis, five of them, shown below, were isolated as interacting with each other.

Key:

Number	Variable
1.	Absence of mother
3.	Contact with mother
4.	Contact with father
7.	Degree of contact with: negative peer group / negative adult role model in community
8.	Severity of conduct disorder

Chart 4: *Diagrammatic representation of clusters showing interaction effect of variables associated with conduct disorder*

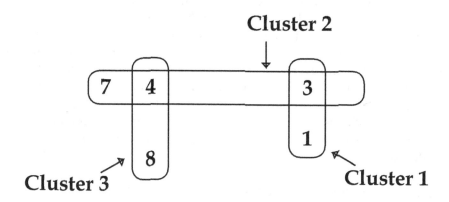

Note: The numbers bear no relation to a weighting or spatial position

Having identified the variables which appeared to affect the development of violent behaviour in the children and adolescents, those variables which interact with each other are presented as clusters within a model (Chart 4).

As shown in this diagrammatic representation, the basic assumptions highlighted by the findings suggest that the most significant interacting variables isolated as contributing to violent and potentially criminal behaviour in the group of adolescents studied were:

- **Cluster 1** – Presence of mother and contact with mother – variables 1, 3
- **Cluster 2** – Degree of contact with mother, degree of contact with father, relationship with peer group – variables 7, 4, 3
- **Cluster 3** – Contact with father and severity of conduct disorder – variables 4, 8

Use of predictive model for early intervention

The information emanating from the findings of this research could have far-reaching implications for curriculum development as well as social and educational policy in terms of models of violence prevention and reduction within the family, school and community, as one could develop what could be termed a predictive model using the above variables to develop effective strategies for prevention and intervention. This would mean therefore that children who have absent mothers or fathers, who have strong relationships with gangs and other negative role models in their communities, as well as youngsters with severe behavioural problems would be considered at risk for violence, and would be pulled out of the system for early intervention. These variables, it is suggested, can be used as a predictive mechanism for children and intervention could therefore prevent the development of later criminal and violent behaviour in adulthood.

Parenting/family and community factors significant

It is interesting to note from the above findings that the theoretical assumptions laid down regarding the role of family and peers and the community were supported in the statistical analyses used and suggested that some of the most significant interacting variables which contributed to violent behaviour in the study cohort of children and adolescents were related to parenting issues. The extent to which these parenting issues may have impacted on the children's behaviour is therefore important in any analysis of the aetiology of the problems and are important in crafting solutions.

Summary

From the discussion in the last two chapters, it is apparent that the impact of violence on children within the context of the entire scenario described above varies in degree by age, gender and level of involvement, depending on whether the children are victims, perpetrators, witnesses, or all of the above. Childredn who are victims include children who are directly involved in violence or are witnesses to violence. Children who are perpetrators, on the other hand, include children who are bullies, those who assault others and show disrespect to authority figures, as well as children involved in extortion of weaker and/or younger children in their schools and communities. Some of these behaviours presented by these children are sometimes referred to as bad behaviour, rudeness, etc. They may, however, be rooted in the nature of parenting these children receive. These factors will be discussed in the following chapter.

It could be argued that some of these social problems are associated directly with the traditional economic problems of high unemployment, under-employment and chronic poverty. There are a number of issues causing children to be victims and perpetrators which are based on the fact that children are in difficult situations due to these systemic problems. When one looks at the emergence of street children and children of migration and child prostitution in Jamaica, for example, though there is an economic basis for these problems, the nature of the problems are such that there appears to be an element of parental compliance and severe neglect of parental responsibility in the creation of these issues (Crawford-Brown 1999). This is in contrast to the definitional framework developed for street and working children in South America where, in countries like Venezuela or Brazil, for example, although street children and child prostitution emerge as a casualty of the economic situation, such children are outside of their normal family structure and go on the streets due to total family breakdown (Crawford-Brown 1989; UNICEF 2000). In terms of migration, there is much less of the "barrel children" phenomenon in the Eastern Caribbean, as families do not see migration as a quick fix to family economic problems. This is possibly due to higher costs of travel, but possibly also due to the presence of traditional Caribbean family values that are not as influenced by metropolitan culture and society as seems to be the case in Jamaica.

As these varied problems have surfaced over the years, increasingly the light of scrutiny has focused on the parents, both mother and father, in terms of their role in solving and coping with some of these problems (Chevannes & Brown 1999). However, much more investigation needs to be done in terms of the contributory role of parents in the actual aetiology of these problems.

The reality of the findings in this chapter in fact suggests that no one factor, but a combination of factors, could be associated with the development of violent behaviour in children and adolescents. The presence or absence of these factors can lead to the deviance, with criminal behaviour being just one form of that deviance. The role of the various functions of parenting therefore keeps emerging over and over again in this chapter as the various issues are dissected. Parenting, as part of the aetiology of violent behaviour in children who are victims and perpetrators, will therefore be discussed in some detail in the next chapter.

CHAPTER THREE

PARENTING AND OTHER FACTORS
Predisposing Children
to Violence

I N order to move beyond the sphere of understanding causative
issues with regard to violent behaviour, it is necessary to develop
effective strategies to intervene effectively to ameliorate the difficulties Jamaican children face as victims. In order to change or modify
the behaviour of those children who are perpetrators, the factors
which predispose these children to violence as victims and as perpetrators must first be identified. Given the discussion in the previous
chapter that points to the role of parenting in promoting or preventing violence against children, it is important to examine all parenting
factors that presently predispose children to violence. These factors
operate at (i) the level of the individual child and the family, (ii) at the
community level, as well as (iii) the broad societal level.

Individual, Family and Parenting Factors

As the issue of violence continues to seriously affect children in
Jamaica, increasingly the light of scrutiny has focussed on the role
of parents, both mothers and fathers, in terms of solving and coping
with some of these problems (Chevannes & Brown 1999). However,
much more investigation needs to be done in terms of the contributory role of parents in the aetiology (cause) of these problems. One
causative variable discussed in the previous chapter which was
related to parenting factors is that of the presence and contact that
children have with their mothers and fathers, as well as the number

of changes in parental arrangements which the child has experienced. This issue brings to the fore the problem of migration of parents and how this phenomenon impacts on the parenting process. This issue was discussed in the previous chapter from the perspective of child. The parenting issues which create problems for children in the migration process will now be addressed.

Parenting and migration: the barrel children syndrome

It is important to note that migration has always been a variable in the matter of child rearing in Jamaica as family kinship networks and systems have traditionally been used as a safety net for children left behind by parents who migrate (Thomas-Hope 1998). However, in the past two decades service agencies and schools working with neglected children have found that increasingly the alternative parental arrangements made for these children are not as stable as they used to be, as grandparents have become younger and busier and are therefore not as available (Barrow 2000). Thus, instead of being left with a stable relative, children are being left in alternative caregiver arrangements or in some cases left on their own.

As discussed in the previous chapter, empirical Caribbean research suggests that in one study done of 70 severely conduct disordered adolescent males remanded in a juvenile correctional facility in Jamaica, contact with father and the absence of mother represented a significant factor associated with the presence and the severity of conduct disorder in that sample population (Crawford-Brown 1993). It is interesting to note that when this study was replicated in 2004 with a larger non-institutionalized conduct disordered adolescent population of 200 children with conduct disorder, absence of mother and contact with father were again found to be two of the most significant variables associated with the most severely conduct disordered subjects. It is important to note that when mothers were found to be absent, the major factors causing the absence of mother was death of mother, migration of mother, low contact with mother related to lack of parental responsibility and abandonment of the child(ren). Low contact with mother related to lack of parental responsibility and abandonment of the children.

Children with emotional and behavioural problems
Lack of adequate resources for provision of holistic mental health services

In a society where there are relatively few social services dedicated to the assessment and treatment of children with emotional and behavioural problems, those children with treatable emotional and behavioural disorders languish in schools, children's homes and other facilities without the appropriate intervention (Crawford-Brown 1993). The state agencies designated to provide therapeutic service have historically never been given adequate resources to intervene effectively with these children's problems, which often include a range of emotional and psychiatric disorders. The budget of these agencies is the first to be cut in the annual trimming of government expenditure and the last to receive funding, thus the systemic issues appear to deteriorate with some.

Lack of parenting education / sensitization of caregivers

Common mental health disorders abound in children in our school systems as well as those in state care (*Sunday Gleaner* February 2010). These disorders include depression, suicidal ideation and unresolved grief reactions which are considered to be emotional problems; autism, which could be considered one of a group of developmental problems; and Attention Deficit Hyperactivity Disorders (ADHD), Conduct Disorder and disorders relating to Oppositional Defiance, which are considered to be behavioural problems. The basic behavioural indicators of these disorders must be understood by parents as well as teachers so that these children can be referred to the appropriate agencies for intervention as soon as possible (Scott 2009). Interventions to treat these conditions have well established protocols internationally, but children in Jamaica often go without assessment and treatment due to lack of access to these all important services in the schools and other social service systems. The provision of basic information to parents, teachers and other community based professionals is essential to ensure adequate referral and disposition of cases.

Gender issues: involvement of women in crime

Another issue that has reflected some changes over time concerns children as victims of serious crimes. The involvement of children is directly related to the involvement of women in crime. The number of women killed as a result of criminal acts was at its highest in Jamaica in 2005 (CCN 2006). Much of these acts of violence against women were, in the estimation of the police, due to reprisal attacks. When gangsters fail to hit their male targets, they sometimes zone in on the targets' female partners and, unfortunately also, their children. The popular rationale for this violent action as stated by one young perpetrator interviewed by this author was "If yu caan ketch Quacko you ketch him shut", meaning if you can't catch the person you want, you catch whoever is closest to him/her. In the mind of one focus group member who was questioned in this matter, this was the reason behind most of the acts of violence where children were murdered. In some cases, criminals would kill the animals or pets belonging to the targeted individual, focus group members reported.[28]

As discussed earlier in this book, the wives, girlfriends, children of criminals or children who are in the vicinity when violent crimes take place become what Harriott (2000) refers to as "soft targets" as criminals cross over the traditional boundaries of gender and age in their lust for revenge, bounty or power. This occurs in turf or gang wars between and within rival factions in Jamaican inner-city communities or in the poor overcrowded slums of rural Jamaica.

Illustration 9: This drawing done by an 8-year-old boy shows a picture of an apparent woman shooting a child. The perpetrator turned out to be a man wearing a woman's wig to commit his crimes.

---

28 Focus group with 26 parents of children attending camp for children with behavioural problems - June 2004

Much less of this kind of criminal activity involving women is seen in the rural areas. In the past two decades, when children were killed violently in these rural areas, these incidents were usually isolated. Anecdotal reports suggested that criminal incidents involving women and children had been associated with family feuds or cases of mental illness (*Daily Gleaner* March 2005), but increasingly police blotters show more frequent incidents in previously untouched rural parishes (see chapter one, p. 28).

Another related issue concerns parents (sometimes mothers as well as fathers) who put their children at risk by becoming perpetrators of violence themselves. This is linked to the issue of changes in parental ethics which is discussed more thoroughly later in this chapter.

In a newspaper report (*Daily Gleaner* October 2006) there was a detailed analysis of this problem, which reported law enforcement officials as saying that there was an increasing trend in Jamaican criminal activity which suggested that women were becoming increasingly involved with dangerous criminals. The report stated that women were involved in the hiding of weapons, and were often used by criminals to sell stolen goods and other spoils of their criminal activities. The extent to which this was done as a result of coercion and fear was discussed as possible reasons for the increasing involvement, but the fact is that these women are involved in crimes involving guns, as collaborators, and perpetrators rather than victims. One deputy police commissioner was reported as suggesting that the women were actually in full support of their gun-toting male partners: "Quite often after men go out to rob, the proceeds of their crimes are passed on to their women, whether for their personal use, or it might be easier for the women to sell those goods as well" (*Daily Gleaner* October 2006).

Women and children: no longer special

There is little empirical evidence to support this, but these anecdotal reports from the police show some evidence of this. It could be argued that even if the numbers are small, the activities of a small number of women put all women at risk. Though the majority of criminal perpetrators continue to be men, the fact that women, and therefore children, who have historically been outside the realm of criminal activity are now involved, creates the perception that women are no longer special and no longer in need of protection. This has now become part of the belief system of the criminal mindset. Children are at risk, therefore, because once women are involved in crime their children are usually not far behind. It is important to note that adolescents in focus group discussions, who grew up in homes where criminal activity (whether perpetrated by mother or father) was common, reported that they grew up with the belief that such activities were normal.

Case study: Consultation between UWI Violence Prevention Programme staff and primary school

I N 2004, one 4-year-old from one urban inner-city community whose father was a known criminal, was the subject of a consultation with the staff of UWIVPP. He reportedly accompanied his father on his nightly criminal activities, and early one morning reported to his mother, "Look on the video and plenty tings me an Daddy tek off the ole lady last night." He was reporting that he and his father had stolen a video and other objects from an elderly woman. When intervention was done through state agencies to take him out of this undesirable situation, where there was obviously gross moral neglect, the professional involved was threatened by the child's father and that professional pulled off the case. This child was never taken away from this undesirable home by the state authorities and continued in this situation for several months. At the time this report was done the child was 7 years old and had begun to abuse his mother who was wheel-chair bound.

Children as means of economic gain

Arising from the previous analysis one sees emerging the fact that some parents (mainly in the lower socioeconomic groups) see their children as a means of economic gain. This is an overriding factor in those child rearing practice situations and one which illustrates aspects of the societal dysfunction mentioned earlier. The following four major issues will further illustrate the extent to which child maltreatment in the Caribbean occurs as a result of inadequacies in this aspect of parenting. As shown in Chart 5, which discusses sexual violence as being a result of an ethical crisis of parenting, the lack of parental ethics is considered a major part of the mindset of some

contemporary parenting styles which lead to child maltreatment and
to such issues as:

(i)   the trading/exchange of children (inter parish and within the
        borders of Jamaica) to known/unknown adults for the purpose
        of increasing the household income

(ii)   parents who pressure children to accept sexual attention from
        adult males and/or to seek sexual attention from adults in
        return for economic favours or material gifts

(iii)   parents who ignore reports of sexual and other abuse from
        children

(iv)   parents whose children are inadequately supervised due to
        migration and/or employment.

These issues will be now be discussed.

Sexual Violence as Ethical Issue of Parenting
Selling/Trading of Children and Child Trafficking: Vigilance Needed

It is important to state that this activity is relatively rare in Jamaica.
There have been isolated incidents of child selling by parents, oftentimes to strangers, mainly in poor rural communities, in exchange for
financial gain. This represents an admittedly small number of cases of
this kind of child maltreatment with parent involvement in Jamaica.
Four cases have been reported to the Child Development Agency
in the past four years. This form of parental behaviour has serious
implications as the reported cases are relatively recent. This would
suggest that the behaviour may give sociologists and social planners
some insight into the shifts in attitudes and the changes in values
and ethics surrounding child rearing practices in Jamaica. In all
cases, when this phenomenon occurred, the behaviour from parents
was associated with major economic deprivation within the family.
It must be recognized, however, that many Jamaican families have
been poor throughout history, but this has not in the past resulted in
the selling of children as an option for the family. In the absence of
data suggesting that rural families are becoming disproportionately
poorer, it appears therefore that this behaviour may signify a change
in parental ethics and value systems, albeit born of difficult economic
circumstances. Given the global climate of international child trafficking, Jamaican authorities must remain vigilant.

Chart 5: *Micro level – sexual violence as ethical issue of parenting*

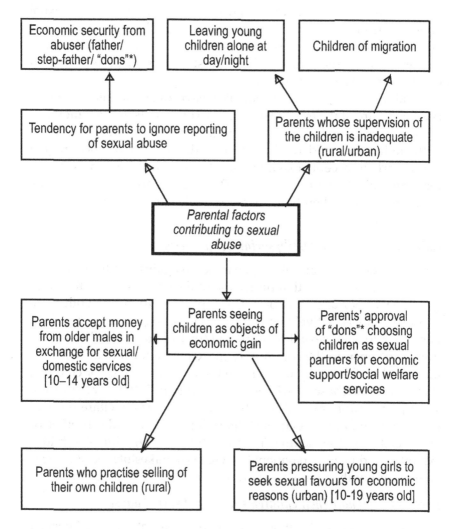

* "dons": community leaders with criminal links

Parents Who Actively Encourage Children to Accept Sexual Attention

Parents who pressure or actively encourage children to accept sexual attention from adults, or who encourage children to seek sexual attention from adults in exchange for economic benefits, is another contemporary issue which appears to stem from a perception that children are important sources of economic gain.

Social services agencies in Jamaica have over the last ten years become aware of the existence of a group of parents, mainly mothers, whose behaviour represents changes in the values associated with traditional child rearing through the activity of encouraging young girls to accept sexual favours from adult males in exchange for economic benefits (Dunn 2002). These parents pressure the children usually when they need economic support to bolster adult contributions.

Children "paying" for family social welfare services

This parental behaviour also appears to go against traditional social norms which stipulate that protection of the child is one of the family's most important functions. These parents, found in both rural and urban areas, actively encourage their young adolescent girls in particular to seek sexual favours and/or to allow sexual advances from adult men in the community in exchange for money, which is then used by the family to maintain the household, e.g. for clothing, shelter and purchase of school supplies (Dunn 2002). Services from adult perpetrators may also include funding social welfare services for the entire family, such as skills training for an older brother or other relative of the victim (Crawford-Brown 1999). Thus the child is exploited and used as payment for what is a makeshift social welfare system for family members based on desperation and survival.

Parents who ignore their children's reports of sexual abuse

As discussed above, the ethics and values of parenting are influenced to a large extent by the community and societal context within which the family exists.

When sexual abuse occurs within the family, i.e. when the perpetrator exists within the home, again children often have little recourse as they are faced with the reality that some parents, particularly mothers, will ignore the sexual abuse of their children despite the evidence, due to the economic dependence of the mother on the perpetrator of the abuse.

It is important to note that the perpetrator (who may be a father, brother or older male relative of the victim, i.e. incest, a stepfather, neighbours or other community members) usually has some influence or power over the mother of the child. The sexual abuse therefore occurs usually when there is a relationship between mother and the child's abuser, where there is power and control on the part of the perpetrator. In some cases, both the mother and the child are victims of physical and sexual abuse. In analysing this particular aspect of behaviour therefore, it is important to look at whether a breach of parental ethics is part of the underlying aetiology of this behaviour.

De-mystification of childhood

This text suggests that the protective role of the family has been discarded by these families, partly because of the apparent de-mystification of childhood and a concomitant lack of respect for the rights of children, which have unfortunately been an ongoing feature of contemporary Jamaican society for some time (Barrow 2001). This de-mystification has been a gradual process, and also speaks to the increasing sexualization of children, which is sanctioned at the community level (e.g. when young children perform highly sexualized dances at community concerts, school functions, etc.)

The de-mystfication of children has also been aided and abetted at the societal level, e.g. when state social service agencies are forced to ignore the plight of hundreds of child victims due to the inadequacy of resources (i) to uphold present state laws, (ii) adhere to policies and procedures regarding parental as well as institutionalized abuse (Milbourn 1998; Crawford-Brown 2000; *Sunday Gleaner* February 14, 2009).

Criminalized families

This breakdown in parental ethics may be a result of economic deprivation as well as the nature of abusive relationships which sometimes exist in what the author will refer to as some "criminalized families". This type of family is one where one member of the parental system is a criminal and is abusive. In that situation, the abuser will criminalize the power and control which occurs in the "normal" abusive family. In this situation, however, the criminal abuser will threaten to kill or harm all members of the extended family of his/her partner, thus ensuring compliance with his/her wishes. These wishes may include sexual "ownership" of a minor child of the abused spouse who the spouse is then powerless to protect.[29] This kind of scenario thus creates a unique situation where the moral judgment of the parent in the cases discussed above is impaired by virtue of the imbalance of power and control that the "criminal spouse" would have on the other.

Parents who do not provide adequate supervision

The final issue which manifests what the author describes as a break-down in the ethics of parenting is inadequate supervision. It is important to note that parents who make the decision to leave their child unsupervised may do so as a result of, for example, a decision to migrate for long-term economic support for the family, or to become a drug courier for short-term economic benefit. There are also cases of neglect that do not involve external migration (Crawford-Brown 2000). On a daily basis, many mothers, due to economic necessity, have to leave children at the mercy of the community in which they live. In most cases, the cultural values of the community allow many of these to survive as the community members take care of these children until their parents return from work, but in some cases, for example, where there is migration of the mother for domestic work, children as young as 2 years old are left to be cared for by siblings a few years their senior.

Child neglect: death by fire

This phenomenon is another situation involving parental neglect and occurs when young children are left alone and unsupervised at night to fend for themselves, particularly in housing situations without safe/adequate electricity, while the parents are involved in employment or otherwise engaged. Again, social service and prevention agencies and practices have found that increasingly children are the victims of neglect where parents make conscious decisions to leave children unsupervised because it is convenient. The safety of children is therefore not apparently in the parental psyche and children some-times die as a result. The data for the past 10 years of children killed violently by fire are relatively consistent as a major cause of death. In 2003 fire was the third largest cause of death of children 0-12 years (CCN 2003). On investigation, increasing numbers of children have

---

29 Focus group discussion with parent group Craig Town - June 2004.

therefore died because parents do not put the safety of their children as a priority.

The ethics of parenting

In most civilized societies, parenting is the single most important task of the family which allows for the effective socialization of its members. Effective parenting therefore ensures the maintenance of a society's cultural integrity, law and order, and the transmission of its values and norms. Parenting skills, however, are often learned, not formally taught; and most individuals with this responsibility have to adapt their parenting styles and direction to meet the changing demands and complex realities of their respective societies as they move through the various transitions of life.

As contemporary Caribbean societies struggle on the path towards meaningful social and economic development as discussed in an earlier chapter, increasingly the social problems and issues which parents face have been made more complex as the impact of social and economic globalization becomes a reality. Throughout the islands of the Caribbean, these social problems, particularly those affecting children and families, have presented serious challenges for social planners and practitioners struggling to find solutions.

It is therefore important to analyse this data within the context of other trends relating to crime and violence in these Caribbean societies and to look at the socioeconomic and psycho-social dynamics of any changes which may be occurring in terms of family organization, structure as well as changes which may be occurring in the other major agencies of socialization which could predispose children to violence.

Chart 6 seeks to present a summary of factors which impact on parents in terms of their role in protecting or encouraging violence against children. The chart can be used to understand the complex nature of the aetiological factors, by looking at the different dimensions of the societal systems which impact on parents. These systems, the chart suggests, intercept to create societal values and attitudes which influence the quality of parenting that children receive. This, the writer suggests, raises ethical concerns regarding parental functioning in Jamaican society.

As shown in the model at Chart 6, this chapter suggests that the changing norms and values at the societal (macro) level have influenced and shaped the changes in values and norms that have

Chart 6: *The ethics of parenting in the family (micro)*

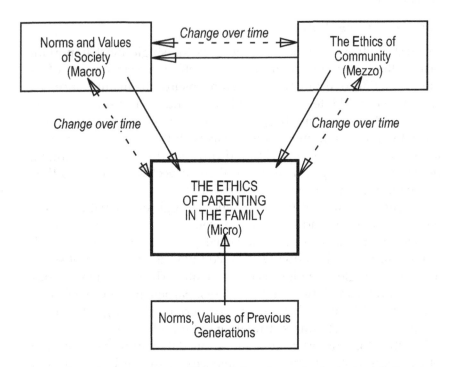

occurred at the community (mezzo) level, particularly in relation to patterns of child rearing and attitudes towards children. This has in turn affected parenting within the family at the individual and small group (micro) level.

Another area of social life affecting parenting negatively relates to community based factors. These will now be discussed in detail.

Community-Based Factors
Pervasiveness of sexual violence as contributory to other violence

The above discussion highlights the fact that the persons who are perpetrators of these forms of violence feed on each other. Thus, this writer argues that there is a thin line between casually abusing a 2-year-old child and killing that child. This suggests that the lack of attention to sexual violence over the years has now created particularly in an adult population that had never learned as children themselves that children are special and need to be protected, as they have been abused sexually and otherwise for years without anyone being accountable. Now that these child witnesses of sexual abuse are adults, and some of them are criminals, it is an easier step for them to kill a child than previous generations of criminals, who at least were socialized in a culture where children were still special, and where media coverage and programming respected and shielded children from explicit sexual content.

The role of the media

The increased coverage of violence in the news media and the proliferation of music videos showing and espousing sexually explicit lyrics have helped to create a crisis of values. When this is factored along with a concomitant absence of formal and accessible channels for helping children and adolescents to process this information in the home, school, or church, a crisis of values and morals is created. One popular song in Jamaican society which describes revenge using guns as a normative way of dealing with childhood poverty was one of the most well liked song by children and adolescents. The role of the media (an important agent of socialization) in possibly fuelling violence is a serious issue pointing to what could be described as a crisis situation that needs to addressed in a holistic manner.

This crisis is reflected in a breakdown in the ethics of parents and consequent breakdown in the values of communities that should be vehicles to pass on the values and mores of previous generations. This situation could therefore be viewed as a cultural phenomenon.

Another issue of violence and exploitation is peer sexual abuse among children where, very often, older children in children's homes physically and sexually abuse younger children in the home. This is a problem that is often not even acknowledged by the staff at the homes or the administration of these facilities.

Issue of corporal punishment in the schools and implications of exposing children to legalized violence

Children in Jamaica and the wider Caribbean are also subject to what UNICEF (2006) describes as "legalized violence" because corporal punishment is considered legal in most Caribbean territories. At a conference of the JTA in April 2006, teachers didn't "buy" the notion of outlawing corporal punishment. They suggested that they were beaten and it did them no harm and that taking away beating from teachers is not the answer. The issue of gender differences regarding

Illustration 10: A child draws a picture of a policeman beating a child at the request of a staffer in a government institution

Illustration 11: This 8-year-old child said his mother choked him when she got angry. What is interesting about this drawing is the mother's seemingly calm exterior.

beating in schools also needs to be discussed in light of the kinds of violence we are seeing emanating from the boys.[30] Boys tend to receive more physical punishment, they report, than girls.

Societal Factors

As shown in the model in Appendix I, the societal factors which predispose the child to violence both as victims and as perpetrators can be identified as those associated with the values and **ethics of parenting** and their relationship to attitudinal changes at the community level in terms of values and norms, as well as issues related to the **marginalization of youth,** a concept explored by Levy (2000) in his discussion of urban poverty and violence in Jamaica. Other societal factors which are at the same time related to community based factors include **economic and psychological dependence** on politicians or community criminal leaders, or anyone who can provide a source of income. The notion that one should depend on someone else, i.e. "the big man" or "the middle class", "Mummie" or "Auntie" could be seen as a psychological mindset of dependence created by the legacy of colonialism which has historically led to deep-seated patterns of **political patronage,** documented historically by Caribbean community development academic Phyllis Coard over three decades ago. These issues can be posited as being part of a rubric of societal dysfunction in aspects of Caribbean society, which have led to changes in the community and family. The macroeconomic issues of **structural adjustment,** as well as the time-worn issues of **poverty, un-employment, and under-employment,** and the inordinately onerous **debt burdens** of Caribbean economies like Jamaica, also result in repercussions at the level of the community. Other factors which have implications for the society include the fact that under-resourced social welfare systems have little access to comprehensive and accessible counselling facilities for needy children, adolescents and their families. This is related to the fact that policies that should be put in place for children to receive these services are not supported by adequate child protection legislation that allows for the provision of wrap-around holistic services. The result is that there is inadequate monitoring of children which allows those in need to fall though the cracks of the social service provisions that do exist.

---

30   Boys in a focus group discussion among boys 8-11 years old.

Lack of adequate enforcement of child protection legislation: Role of the Office of Children's Advocate/Child Development Agency

Data on the prevalence of sexual abuse against children have resulted in social planners for years asking for strengthened legislation to ensure that perpetrators of abuse and neglect do not go unpunished. Now the long awaited Child Care and Protection Act which provides for this is in place in Jamaica. However, the reality is that it is possible that the legislation is too little too late, in view of the fact that almost the entire young adult population has grown in a society where it has been seen as alright to abuse children sexually and otherwise. To change these attitudes will require massive expenditure by the Child Development Agencies on "in your face" public education advertising using aggressive marketing strategies to get adults in the age group 20 to 24 to really understand that sexual abuse of chidren is wrong. So far, having the Act has meant little change in terms of attitudes towards the sexual abuse of children. So, although the law exists, it has been labelled "toothless" by many practitioners. Policy makers have therefore underestimated the resources needed to educate and inform the general population regarding the serious implications of sexual abuse. Frequent consultations and "talk shops" to discuss the issues are important, but money must be put into community based multimedia programming such as billboards, television advertising and other mass media, with the help of the Office of Children's Advocate to assist parents and the community at large develop over time a zero-tolerance approach to sexual abuse in any form. (See billboard prototype, Photo 5.)

The de-mystification of childhood

The de-mystification of women has been followed by the de-mystification of childhood. When coupled with the epic-like proportions of sexual crimes against women and children as discussed earlier in the text, children are put at even greater risk at all levels of the society. The unusual cases of children under 5 and infants being killed, are all a part of this grim picture, which must be addressed in a holistic way by multiple levels of intervention.

The brutality and the viciousness of these acts of violence have literally numbed Jamaican and regional practitioners and policy makers. Little empirically based research, however, has been done to first track the mortality rates in terms of the non-accidental killings of our children or to gain an understanding of the psycho-social dynamics of their motives. This kind of information would help in the development of interventions Without this kind of information, which is within the purview of forensic psychologists and forensic social workers, interventions will be forever short-lived and ad hoc, creating very little meaningful change in the macro situation over time.

Children as victims of violent culture

Violence against children such as murder can be seen as an extension of other forms of violence within a subculture where violence is seen as a normal method of conflict resolution. The inability of the state to protect the children and hold individuals accountable for exploitation of children is another contributing factor to this problem. The case of an 11-year-old girl in rural Jamaica, whose 17-year-old abusive cousin referred to her publicly as his "sexual slave" without being held accountable is an example of the failure of the state's ability to protect its children in a meaningful way. The perpetrator had developed his plan from unsupervised viewing of cable television.

Photo 5: Posters like this sponsored by the private sector could be used as billboards to sensitize the public to the plight of children who are at risk for accidental or intentional harm and injury.

(Adapted with permission from Ceasefire Chicago)

Illustration 12: This picture was drawn by a 12-year-old girl who illustrated the commonplace nature of gun violence in her community, which was often in close proximity to houses within communities. Innocent civilians, including children, are therefore often unwitting victims

Illustration 13: This picture, the little 6-year-old girl explained, represents the trees shooting at people on the street. (What this little girl had not realized was that the gunman in her community often used the trees for cover and climbed into the trees at night to shoot at his victims. It took some processing for her to lose her fear of trees)

Children as support services to criminal culture

Children continue to be "soft targets" in drug wars, particularly in urban communities, as the increase in gun trafficking continues. When there are more guns, there are more shootings, and young children get caught in the crossfire, by virtue of their innate vulnerability. The proximity to guns in their homes and communities also predispose them to become gun couriers and provide support services to the criminal culture, such as "gun watching" and "spotting individuals" as targets. This is unacceptable and is inherently preventable.

Illustration 14: A 10-year-old girl from an urban community in Jamaica and a 12-year-old boy's drawings of guns illustrate the stark reality that our children are in close association with guns and other weapons

One of the most common findings in working with children living in violent communities in Jamaica, is the way in which they are able to draw very detailed pictures of guns. In these pictures (Illustration 14) the children were doing a poster to warn other children not to play with guns. It is to be noted that guns are not sold in Jamaica and most guns are smuggled into the country.

Lack of database/Role of Child Abuse Registry

The absence of a comprehensive and accurate database on all forms of child abuse, including sexual abuse has been, for decades, a huge obstacle to combating the problem of sexual violence against children effectively. In a 2004 news report, the Coalition of the Rights of the Child lamented the absence of a Child Abuse Registry in a situation where the then new Child Care and Protection Act required mandatory registration of child abuse. Another problem is that parents (mothers included) were not reporting the cases of sexual violence to the authorities.

One of the deterrents to this is the problem that sexual violence against women and children has become so acceptable and commonplace that it has developed into one of the social ills arising from the "ah nuh nutten" [it is nothing] syndrome.[31] Thus, parents who would previously go to a clinic for help and report the abuse no longer do this for reasons that are simplistic and reflect a change in community values and attitudes, which are discussed in detail in chapter six. Some of the issues, however, are presented briefly as follows:

• Mothers who know their children are being abused do not want to act due to dependence on the male
• The perpetrators are often from the criminal elements in their communities and the mother and child may be threatened if they report the abuse
• Sexual violence is used as an element of power and control in adult relationships and so children learn this early and grow to accept actual violence as normal

Ease of access to illegal weapons

As shown in Figure 16 below, the gun is the weapon of choice most frequently used in murders, accounting for 76% of the murders in 2004. It is important to note that the majority of these guns are not produced locally, nor are they easily available through gun shows, etc., as exists, for example, in other parts of the world, and therefore almost all of the murders recorded using guns were committed with the use of illegal weapons. Ease of access to illegal weapons by perpetrators is therefore a significant factor which predisposes children to being a victim of violence. In a scenario where community criminals know few other alternatives to violence as a means of conflict resolution, children therefore again become easy targets.

---

31 Jamaican vernacular describing phenomena which are usually seen as inconsequential.

Figure 16: *Weapons used in murders (2004)*

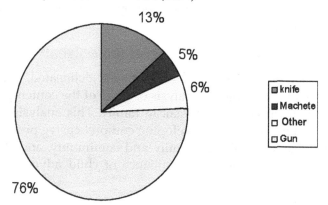

Summary

Children and their family functioning: microcosm of their society

In order to investigate and understand the impact of violence on children and families, it is important to note that children within the context of their families must be seen as being a microcosm of the society in which they live and function. The impact on them as a group will be a reflection of its impact on the society at large. In evaluating its impact, therefore, it is useful to look at the different types of violence in the society generally, the nature of that violence as it affects children, and the trends indicated by that data over time.

This text posits that changes at the societal macro level and at the level of the community may affect the effectiveness of the individual's parenting process. It is also argued that a range of factors are at the root of the aetiology of the problem of poor parenting. These factors include (i) changes in the economic function and viability of the family as well as (ii) changes at the mezzo level in the community, creating informal alternative child welfare services outside of the state. Changes are also occurring at the community level in terms of the perceptions of child-rearing responsibilities. The lack of change at the macro/societal level in terms of inadequacies and lack of teeth in the legislation for the protection of children has also given new dimensions to the challenges facing families. These have created a situation where there appears to be a shifting of some of the traditional values and ethical guidelines being used by parents and other care-givers to raise their children.

Inadequate and unacceptable levels of professionals

It appears that given the kinds of problems delineated, there is need for in-depth sociological analysis of some of the contemporary child-rearing practices of the Jamaican family. This analysis needs to be done as a precursor for developing comprehensive prevention programmes based within the family and community, and should be monitored by an independent alliance of child advocates and professionals.

There is also need for massive public education and support programmes for existing parenting agencies to provide parenting support and to address the issue of effective parenting, in addition to providing and strengthening state social support systems via paraprofessionals for families with dependent children, who are also at risk in terms of economic and social deprivation.

The issue of penalties for parental neglect must also be addressed. Stiffer penalties will have to be put in place as a deterrent to protect children and reinforce societies' mandate to protect its children. It is important to note, however, that cases of neglect will have to be investigated thoroughly by professionals to determine the difference between actions based on neglect versus poverty, as there appears to be some link between economic deprivation and some forms of neglect. The important issue, however, is that the problem must be confronted and dealt with at all levels of the society by competent and well trained professionals. Case loads of 400 children per professional social worker is an unacceptable and untenable state of affairs.

Failure to act on these very critical issues can only lead to a breakdown in the agencies of socialization and a consequent deterioration in the quality of life of our society as we know it.

"IN THEIR OWN WORDS"
Children speak out about violence
in their environment

T H E pictures in this chapter were selected from over 200 pictures used in the assessment of children in Jamaica and Trinidad and Toabgo who attended specialized treatment sessions for children at risk for violence between 2004 and 2006.

This chapter with its graphic pictures captures a view of the children's world from their own perspective. The following words of a 10-year-old girl present a view of Jamaica in a poem entitled "My World".

MY WORLD

If you listen to this world
What do you think you'd hear?
I think you'd hear it crying out in anguish, sorrow and fear,
You wouldn't even notice the joy and laughter here,
You would hear it crying out in anguish, sorrow and fear.
If you looked into this world,
What do you think you'd see?
You'd see the poverty staring in your faces,
You wouldn't see the joy, warmth, or all the happy places,
You would just see the poverty staring in your faces.
If you could touch this world,
What do you think you'd feel?
I think you'd feel the harshness of the people living here,

You wouldn't feel the tenderness, the warmth or the love,
You'd just feel the harshness of the people living here.

— © January 1994 N. Brown

Note: Please note demographic information and locations have been removed to protect the identity of the children.

Community Violence

001 – "Don't kill me please!" –The drawing above was done by a 10-year-old girl who lives in a violent inner-city community of Kingston. She was returning from church with her mother when she witnessed the stabbing death of a man. She spontaneously begged the killer to spare the man's life, saying, "God would not make you go to heaven." The perpetrator then threatened to kill her. Her mother pleaded for her daughter's life, stating that she was a bright girl, waiting to do her GSAT exams. The killer spared her life, but the little girl was very traumatized for several months after the incident

002 – *"Watch me an yuh"* – 11-year-old boy attending a day programme for at risk youth drew his vision of "What violence means to me in my community" based on violence in his community. He depicts incidents of physical violence, drive-by shooting and domestic violence

003 – *"Me a go kill yu"* – This 8-year-old girl's drawing shows her feeling that she would kill anyone who tried to rape her

004 – *"Rape! No! Help me!"* – This adolescent 13-year-old girl graphically illustrates a range of violent activities in the community in which she lives, including attempted rape, an accident on the road, and the use of stones to hit someone in the head. This picture also shows an altercation between a man with a knife threatening to kill a woman who uses a broken bottle to defend herself

Note the child's depiction of a zinc fence, a material used as a housing boundary in many inner-city communities in urban Jamaica.

005 – *"Give me your bag"* – In this picture, an 11-year-old girl illustrates the experience of going to the shop for her mother and being accosted by a gunman. This brave girl told him no, but she was very scared as he held the gun to her head. She was very worried that she would die by a bullet to her forehead just like a friend's death she had witnessed

006 – *"Someone help me!"* – This is an 11-year-old girl's depiction of violence witnessed by her. The constant cries for help she hears from women in her family and community was striking

007 – "Clappers gun is an early start for gunmen" – During a community intervention by the UWI Violence Prevention Programme in one urban community in 2004, a 14-year-old boy did this poster. The drawing spoke to a "children's war" which had developed between children from different parts of a polarized community. The handmade weapons were used to mimic the activities of gunmen in their community which included the kidnapping of one child and retaliation for perceived wrongs. One such "shooting" led to one child severely injuring her eye

008

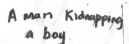

009

008 – *"Somebody kidnapping me"* and **009** *A man kidnapping a boy* – These pictures were taken from drawings by children in Trinidad and Tobago in 2005. They belong to urban communities and produced these drawings as part of a small camp held for children at risk for violence. The drawings represent the fear expressed by children at the time when there was a rash of kidnappings of children, allegedly connected to the drug trade

A picture of my daddy dying - Age 4 boy

Stop kid

8/4/05

Age 4 Male

010 – *"My father getting shot"* – This 4-year-old graphically describes his father's death in this picture. On his first day at the UWI Violence Prevention Clinic, he cried loudly demanding a red marker, which he explained was necessary to show his father's death, to show the blood he saw – describing it as a man punching him in his belly with a loud sound. His siblings confirmed that his father was in fact shot

011 – *"My uncle getting shot in the bus"* – This 7-year-old boy describes traumatic experiences of his uncle getting shot in a bus

012 – *"Children a bruk fight in my school"* – This 12-year-old child, frequently extorted money from 6-year-olds in his school. Here he shows constant fighting on the playground.

013 – *"Gun shooting in my community"* – This 12-year-old little girl expressed the fear of guns going off constantly in her community near her home

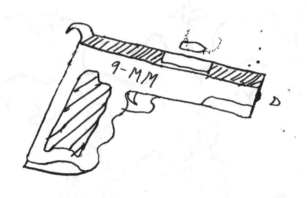

014

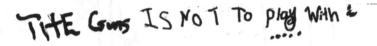

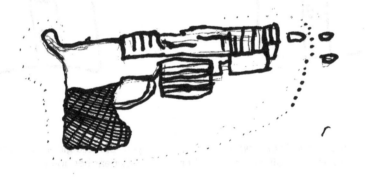

015

014-015 – *"One of my father's guns"* – The extreme detail of these drawings by a 12-year-old boy and a 10-year-old girl leads one to the conclusion that the guns were a part of these childrens' immediate environment.

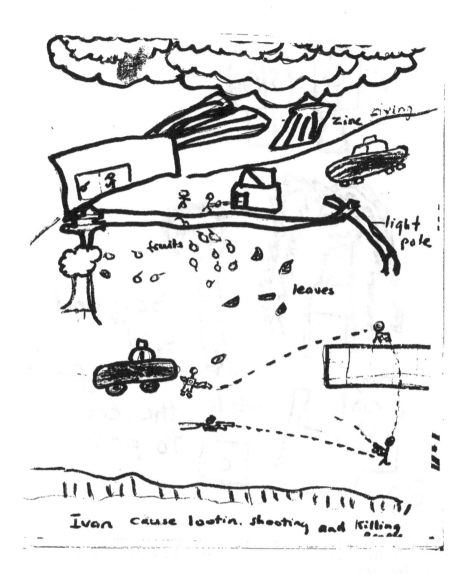

016 – "Gunman shooting and looting my fadder tings in Hurricane Ivan" – This 12-year-old boy's picture shows how children associate gun violence with hurricanes, where there is looting when the family goes to a shelter.

Author's note: The possibility of looting causes many families in the inner city to stay at home during a natural disaster, rather than go to a shelter.

017 – *"The day my best friend get lick down by a car"* – Children as witnesses to road violence: This 6-year-old lost her friend to a hit-and-run accident in front of her school

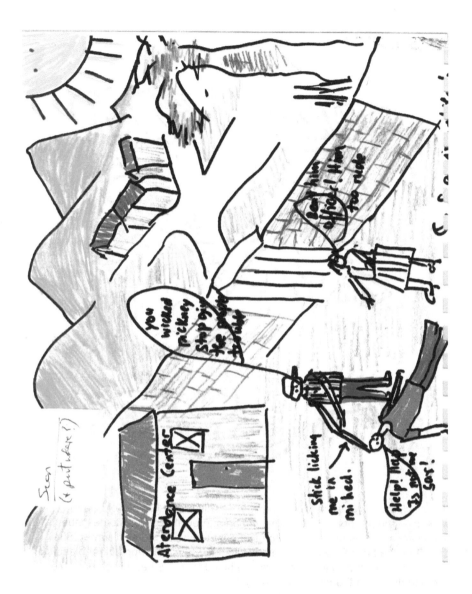

018 – "*Beat him officer! Him too rude.*"– This 15-year-old boy's picture shows an example of institutional abuse in an agency set up to protect children who are at risk for violence. The child shows a uniformed police officer beating him with an implement as a response to a complaint by a staff member. Too often, the agencies set up to protect and rehabilitate youngsters abuse the children in their care further compounding their behavioural disorders

Severe Childhood Trauma

019 – *"My heart ripped in two by the gun"* – This bright 10-year-old, who witnessed the murder of her family members, drew this picture to describe her feelings. She exhibited symptoms of post-traumatic stress disorder. She describes the bullets from the gun that killed her family as ripping her bleeding heart in two. As shown in the picture, the blood from her heart is causing the dog and the cat in the foreground to fight

Author's Note: In order to prevent the development of further pathology, it is important that this child be referred to the appropriate mental health agency. Though this was done, the parent refused to take the child there because of the stigma associated with that agency.

020 – *"I am the devil, I love to kill people"* – This 10-year-old boy drew this picture to express his feelings about his mother and his world. To the left is a picture of himself and his mother crying, and to the right is the picture of himself as the devil with a pitchfork

Author's Note: This child's drawing hinted at a possibly serious psychological problem, but follow up and tracking of this child was not possible despite referrals to the Child Guidance Clinic. Limited resources of the Violence Prevention Programme hindered any effective follow up, much to the frustration of the professionals concerned.

021 – *"I want my mommy"* – This 7-year-old girl shows the fear she experienced when she was trapped in a gun battle between the police and gunmen in her community

022 – "*I love my daddy so mush*". – This picture was drawn by a 10-year-old boy living in urban Jamaica, whose father was murdered in his presence. In this case, the murder of one man killed one man, but it also killed the boy's sense of his own identity. The boy wrote the following words to his father (in the drawing): *"I love my Daddy so mush and he is the best Daddy in the world, and I love him so mush and every day he give me lunch money to go to school."*

023 – *"Don't touch me."* – This 10-year-old girl depicts the plight of many children and women who are consistently harassed on the streets by adult males; this sometimes includes touching as shown in the drawing

024 – *"My mother's death "* – This 7-year-old girl describes in great detail the events surrounding the death of her mother.

Author's note: It is important that young children not be given too much information surrounding the death of a loved one, particularly if the details could be traumatic to the child. Children who experience sudden loss need stronger support. One visit by school officials is not enough to help children cope with serious traumatic events. There must be follow up for at least 3-6 months, or more if necessary.

025 – *"My mother's funeral"* – This 7-year-old girl describes in great detail the funeral of her mother.

Author's note: It is generally good for children to be a funerals, but young children should be helped to understand what is happening at each stage of the funeral and burial process

026 – *A man with locks shooting a little pickney*: This 9-year-old boy draws a picture of the man who shot his baby sister. He calls the man by name

Author's note: this drawing was done on a field trip near to a popular cemetery in a rural area. He nonchalantly described his sister's death and her killer.

Domestic Violence

027 – *"Father beating mother"* – This 6-year-old girl who presented with academic and behavioural problems, revealed in her drawing what she could not speak about in a therapeutic session with either of her parents present

028 – *"We want peace. My mother squeezing my neck"* – Boy 8 years old –
An 8-year-old boy describes physical abuse by his mother. Note the smile on
the face of his mother while he is being abused.

029 – *"I feel to rape her"* – The use of a gun to rape a child was documented in a matter of fact manner by a 10-year-old girl

030 – *"I am not her man. I am her son"* – This drawing by a very intelligent 10-year-old boy in Kingston documents the seemingly rare practice of mother/son incest and struggles he experienced in dealing with the emotions it evoked

031 – *"Don't tell, nobody will believe you"* – This picture depicts the case of an 11-year-old girl who drew the voice of her father who kept repeating the words in her mind. She exhibited severe anger and frustration as her mother never believed her. This is a common problem when women are totally economically dependent on their male partners. Women therefore feel forced to stay with the men, even though they are abusing their child

032 – *A hearing-impaired child "speaks" out.* – This drawing by a 6-year-old girl, who was unable to hear or to speak, played a key role in prosecution of the perpetrator

033 – *Peer Abuse – 6-year-old perpetrators*: This drawing by a 6-year-old boy who tried to rape an eight year-old girl in collaboration with two other six year olds. This child was over exposed to adult sexual practices, due to pornographic films being shown in a yard. His mother regularly attended this public showing with a younger sibling.

Note: The parents in this group seemed not to understand the impact of children regularly witnessing these adult sexual activities.

034 – *Use of the cell phone and the gun* – This picture done by a 15-year-old girl illustrates the role of the gun in sexual abuse of children. The presence of the cell phone to document the act was of particular concern

035 – *"Mi a go rape you."* – This picture done by a 10-year-old shows the link between sexual exploration and gun violence which was never expressed verbally by children, but kept appearing time and time again in their art work. This represents a contemporary spin on child abuse which is worrying

036 – *The undeveloped problem of male-male child abuse.* The explicit nature of picture by an 8-year-old illustrates details regarding the difference between a predator expression of joy, and the face of the suffering child

037 – *"Sen on yu pickney tonight"* – This drawing by a 13-year-old girl clearly documents her knowledge of the practice of hoodlums who intimidate mothers regarding the sexual abuse of their children in exchange for food and other social welfare needs

THE EFFECT OF VIOLENCE on Children in Jamaica: The 'Ah Nuh Nutten' Syndrome

V I O L E N C E in its various forms has been taking a heavy toll on the physical, emotional and mental health of Jamaican children, who exhibit symptoms of depression, post-traumatic stress disorder, aggressive and impulsive behaviours, difficulty concentrating, bedwetting, and attachment problems. It is important to note that many of these symptoms exist within the context of unstable familial environments and are factors that are associated with aggressive and delinquent behaviours (Samms-Vaughan 2005), further fuelling our present epidemic of violence. A study in 2002 by the Ministry of Health in Kingston and St. Andrew concluded that 25% of adolescents do not feel 100% safe in their communities (Gayle 2004) and 30% of adolescents in the study indicated that they worry about fighting and violence in their homes and communities. The impact of violence on children, therefore, will vary depending on the type of violence they experience. The following discussion will look at (i) the social impact of this violence on children, (ii) the impact on their educational and leisure activities, (iii) the impact of the media in promoting violence, (iv) the economic impact of violence as it affects children, and (v) the psychological impact of violence on children.

Social Impact

Violence is one of the major factors leading to a poor quality of life for many of Jamaica's children, and one that ultimately leads to their marginalization. The fact is that, as shown in Figure 17, and discussed previously, many of our children are caught up in the ongoing "crossfire" of various types of violence in Jamaican society. The term "crossfire" refers to a symbolic barrage of the different forms of violence which interact with each other, with gruesome consequences (Crawford-Brown 2003).

As shown in the diagram, the different types of violence emanate and ricochet from the various systems that interface and intercede in the life of the child, at the level of the home and family, the community and the society. As discussed in earlier chapters, in some households and communities, child abuse and neglect, particularly sexual abuse, have reached epidemic proportions. In a survey of 100 children from primary and secondary corporate area schools with behavioural problems seen by the UWI Violence Prevention Programme in 2004, 20% of the children reported that they were bullied or had bullied other children. In that same year, in rural Jamaica, violence caused the closure of some schools, and children were prevented from preparing for examinations in rural and some parts of urban Jamaica (UNICEF 2006). The same report suggested that others had to be escorted to examination centres by the police, and that in some of the schools in communities where there were high levels of violence, the attendance and performance declined. Outside of school, children in the most troubled communities of urban Jamaica could not go about freely nor speak openly about their fear, as gunmen move from one house to another intimidating families and killing, sometimes randomly, sometimes in a predetermined manner.

" M E an my brother dem did tink it was firecrackers dem was bursting, because we never really hear gunshot so close before. My father, he got shot in the middle of him forehead. Him did talk to me before him ded. Him sey, Everyting goin be allright. Me shake mi mother but she couldn't sey anyting. She did ded already. Dem shoot my big sista too. Dem did kill her. She was lying in the bed beside me, but dem never shoot me an mi two brothers. We stay wid dem till mawnin when de neighbours come. Dem did fraid to come before daylight and dem did tink sey all a we did ded. Mi uncle tek we an look after we. Afterwards, mi auntie sey de gunman dem did leave a paper sey dem sorry, it was de wrong house, dem did mek a mistake." (Age 11 – Kingston)

Figure 17: *Summary of community discussion on violence using Participatory Learning Activity technique (PLA)*

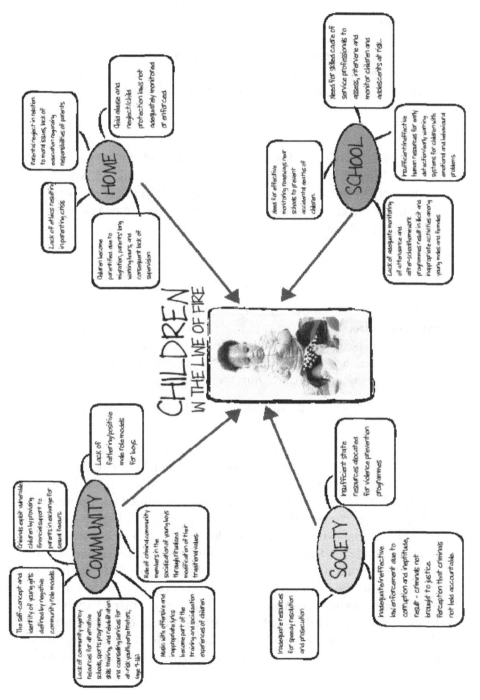

> "Miss, mi see more dan 10 people ded in my community, but not as much as 20 miss."
> "How do you feel? Do you feel scared sometimes?"
> "No miss, Mi use to it miss. **Ah nuh nutten miss.**"
> (The latter phrase means "it is nothing" and is used frequently by children seen at the UWI Violence Prevention Clinic.)

> " T H E Y came in the middle of the night. My father got shot. They kill my Mommy too, an my sista. She was 15. Me neva cry because Mommy did teach Cary (11 year-old brother) how to cook scramble egg, so me know sey we wouldn't starve, but Cary did cry."

Negative community role models as agents of socialization

In the community, some self-imposed community leaders routinely exploit children in various ways by providing assistance to parents in the form of social welfare services. For example, as discussed earlier, they pay the cost of school fees, uniforms and books to parents in exchange for sexual favours from their children.

Role the state as safety net for families usurped by community leaders

it is the responsibility of the state to provide assistance to needy children and their families. Failure to adequately create this safety net has therefore created a vacuum, which has been filled by these "community leaders", some of them having criminal backgrounds.

The State is contributing to violence against children by default, therefore, to the extent that the policies that have been put into place to protect children from instances of the violence cited above are not enforced operationally on the ground. Policies are therefore largely ineffectual to the extent that the State has not exerted its authority and power sufficiently through its law enforcement capabilities, its agencies, and its designated agents to protect children from the different forms of violence which affect them in their daily lives. Children are not protected in basic areas, such as on the streets and in the buses that take them to and from school, where they are vulnerable to sexual and other predators who steal their personal belongings, primarily watches, cell phones, laptops, as well as their lunch monies and bus fares at will.

Implications of illegal, informal transportation systems

On the buses and taxis in which children travel daily to and from school, they continue to be exposed to inappropriate auditory and visual sexually explicit material in illegal taxis and mini-buses that constantly challenge the legitimate systems set up for public transportation.

From the above discussion, it is apparent that Jamaican children are not protected from violence in their society and, in addition, when they get into trouble, sometimes through no fault of their own. For example, when there is parental or other adult complicity and instruction in criminal acts, they are not given the ameliorative or rehabilitative services that they need.

Impact on Educational and Leisure Activities

When children experience violence at such concentrated levels, in so many "doses", and from so many different directions, they are affected holistically, that is, emotionally, psychologically and cognitively.

This situation therefore undermines their ability to be educated as well as their access to the education that is available. One World Bank report in 2003[32] found that when they compared Jamaica to seven other Caribbean countries, Jamaica had the highest secondary completion rate, but Jamaican children exhibited the lowest number of classroom hours, as well as the lowest average performance in CXC results in Mathematics and English. The report suggested that this may have been due to frequent school closures due to violence and civil disturbances in some areas. In 2003-2004 one local newspaper report stated that violence caused school closures in Kingston, Spanish Town and Montego Bay for more than two days. Other schools were closed due to poor security conditions (*Daily Gleaner* June 10, 2005).

As a result of violence in their communities, children are often prevented from going to school or attending other leisure activities such as camp or after school programmes. In one community in

---

32 Cited in **UNICEF Report on Children and Violence in Jamaica** (2006).

the summer of 2005, a social worker from one of the major peace promotion programmes (the Peace Management Initiative) in one inner-city community, had to intervene directly to get the cooperation of one set of criminals to halt the gunfire long enough to allow a group of children to cross a road in the community so the children could attend a summer camp. It is possible that much of the behaviour of these gangs as it relates to children, is part of a battle for the symbols of power and control and is often not maliciously directed at the children themselves. However, until these gangs and their behaviour can be controlled, children will continue to remain easy targets and victims.

Impact of the Media: Glorification of Violence

As discussed in previous chapters the worldview towards most of the children who were involved in the various interventions with the author for this project was that violence was a way of life. As discussed much of this has been reinforced by public media as well as the entertainment sector of the media. Through glorification of violence in the media, as evidenced by the sensational reporting of crime and violence in the electronic and printe media in particular, Jamaican children have become too comfortable with violence in all its forms. Most state violence prevention policies globally guard against the glorification of violence by all forms of media.[33] When media houses in Jamaica have massive media coverage of the funerals of notorious criminals, or when the reporting of criminal acts show the graphic footage of bodies of victims in prime family time news programming, this creates an atmosphere which predisposes children to trauma as well as the numbing of their own responses to violence.

Role of popular music: need for ongoing monitoring to determine media worthiness

jamaicans are internationally recognized for their love of music, and music and dance could be described as being built in to the DNA of all Jamaicans and, in fact, that of all Caribbean peoples. The high regard, bordering on "reverence", with which many child clients aged 0-12 years had for songs containing very violent lyrics is, however, a cause for concern as the music and its rhythms it would seem, are

---

33 Centre for Disease Control (CDC), *Violence Prevention Policy* (Atlanta, Georgia: CDC).

being used by entertainers to convey antisocial messages. When one considers that the children hearing and internalizing these lyrics are as young as two to four years old, the implications of this for early socialization are serious. Given the above discussion on the impact and the power of the media, it would seem that recent demands by the Jamaican Broadcasting Commission for regular screening of popular music in the market by media personnel and child advocates to determine what is fit for air play is timely.

In Jamaica, where a culture based on the normalization of violence as a way of life in dealing with any and every conflict has been internalized by this generation, too many parents and adults are unaware of the nature of the lyrics of these songs, and disregard its impact on their children. Music played in prime time for young children and families must be closely monitored for content appropriate for children, as the plethora of songs which espouse the values of rape and the abuse of women as part of a normal male-female interaction, is worrying. Criminals who commit vicious and violent crimes, and who make money through various forms of entertainment while in prison also give the wrong message to at risk youths.

A song by one such perpetrator meant to one at risk youth that "rape was not necessarily a bad thing because the singer, who had been serving time for that crime, was making money from the experience."[34] The society must therefore be careful about the ethical procedures involved in paying criminals during, and after, the rehabilitation process.

Economic Impact

The economic impact of violence is tremendous, as UNICEF's country office in Jamaica estimates that violence costs the country over US$236 million or J$15 billion annually.[35] It is important to note that this figure is equivalent to the entire budget of the Ministry of Health. The reduction of violence, generally, and against children in particular, would therefore be of economic benefit to the cash starved financial system within the Jamaican economy. An even more significant economic factor is the waste of human resources caused by the unnecessary loss of human life.

---

34 Focus group discussion: At risk boys (ages 8-16), Grants Pen, St. Andrew, Jamaica, 2004.
35 Situation Analysis of Women and Children in Jamaica, UNICEF Update 2007.

It is important to note, however, that the consequences of not providing the necessary preventive, ameliorative or rehabilitative services will put additional strains on the Jamaican economy in terms of the millions of dollars needed. Apart from the negative impact of violence on the emotional health of the nation, the fact that the quality of life of the citizens of the country are impacted is worthy of note and must be seen as part of the cost of this difficult situation.

The young people of Jamaica, who have grown up in a culture of violence have normalized and glorified much of the violence that is reflected in the media, and have incorporated it into their lives without much acknowledgement by the state that this poses serious problems for the society's future. One must be cognizant of the macro implication of the impact of violence, which is insidious. More than two generations of youngsters have grown up in a society that has developed dysfunctional interpersonal patterns in their relationships as it relates to violence against women and children, and as it relates to their understanding of their world.

This value system and world view is in direct contrast to Jamaicans just one or two generations ago, who grew up in similar economic circumstances but had strong and sound value systems based on traditional values of respect for children, women, the elderly and for the institution of the family.

A 1 2 -year-old boy driving through an upper class community in Kingston, Jamaica:

"Miss, how come the house dem up here don't have no fence?"

"That's how they are built, dear. They have lawns and flowers.?"

"Den, what dem do when gunman start fi fire shot, miss? Dem supposed to have on zinc fence to protect dem from the bullet dem, miss."

(Violence Prevention Programme, "A Breath of Fresh Air": Summer Camp 2004 for children from communities at risk for violence)

Psychological Impact: Over-exposure to Violence and Trauma

The psychological impact that violence has on children is difficult to quantify as its impact is so insidious and far-reaching. The children's words speak for themselves:

> **A 1 2** -year-old child reported to have killed a dog, speaking to his counsellor in the UWI Violence Prevention Programme (Mona & St. Augustine Social Work students):
> *"Because him bite mi on mi bumsie miss."*
> "How did you kill him?"
> *"Mi ketch him wid food, miss. Den I tie him, an den I drown him miss.*
> "So how did you feel when you were drowning the dog?"
> *"Mi feel sorry for him, miss."*
>
> (Trinidad and Tobago Summer camp for children at risk for violence Summer 2005)

A survey on the impact of violence on children done in 2005 found that 80% of the children surveyed in two inner-city schools in a violence prone area of Kingston had witnessed five to eight murders or had known five to eight murder victims (Crawford-Brown 2006). Ten per cent (10%) of them had witnessed less that 5 murders and 10% had witnessed more than 8 murders.[36] The research interviewed 115 children drawn from two primary schools in violence prone areas of Kingston.

Children vulnerable to school based violence

Areas of particular vulnerability to the psychological impact of violence are the schools, where the fear of kidnapping created some concern in Trinidad and Tobago in 2004. In Jamaica, this problem has recently reared its "ugly head". For years the stage had been fight-

---

36 It is to be noted that quantitative, as well as qualitative methods were used to do this crude survey (counting by a show of hands) in a focus group. The results were subjectively determined by the children themselves and, consequently, the findings cannot be used to generalize to a wider population of urban children in Jamaica. In one case, a child reported that he had witnessed *"plenty, plenty more than nine, miss, but not as much as 20"*.

ing, where older youths from within the school as well as from the community have become a part of the conflicted environment in some schools. Many of these schools had largely tolerated or ignored these incidents for years, across the social classes, concentrating on academic issues and ignoring the social and psychological problems underlying these behaviours. Incidents of bullying, extortion, teasing and frequent fighting, have now become more prevalent and are now more savage in nature.

O N E 17-year-old boy who had killed a 6-year-old girl, when questioned as to whether he felt remorse on seeing the child's picture, answered, *"No miss, she was just a cockroach, miss."* This child had been brain-washed by a community criminal who had de sensitized him about his crime, to the point where he saw his victims as no longer human. (This phenomenon is often seen in war zones such as Iraq and Afghanistan as well as with child soldiers in Africa). (CNN Report "Children of Islam", August 16, 2009)

Based on an analysis of over 400 cases seen at the UWI Violence Prevention Programme for the four-year period (2002-2006, the writer sought to develop a typology of behaviour which could reflect the impact that traumatic incidents of violence have had on children, particularly in urban Jamaica. This is presented in the model (Chart 7, p. 142).

" I   would like to know what it feels like to kill somebody"
– male, age 12

What is trauma?

Trauma can be described as an event in which a person has experienced or has been confronted with an event or events that involve actual or threatened death or serious injury. Trauma can also be caused by a threat to the physical integrity of the self or others, and is usually associated with responses such as intense fear, helplessness or horror.

The effect of trauma

Traditionally, children who are traumatized may develop a range of psychological disorders, which can run the gamut of the Diagnostic Statistical Manual of Mental Disorders. The most common of these described in the literature globally include disorders such as Post-Traumatic Stress Disorder or Disrupted Attachment Disorder (Osofsky 2004).

It is to be noted that traumatic incidents experienced by the children and adolescents interviewed by the writer involved (i) children who were victims of gun violence where their parents or close relatives had been killed, in many cases in their presence, or (ii) children who had been sexually abused and, to a lesser extent, (iii) children who had been physically and emotionally abused.

> *A 7-year-old* boy speaking to his counselor.....
> Child: *"Miss, me like it when we have war in my community"*
> Counselor: "Why do you like the war, dear?"
> Child: *"Miss, me like the war because plenty people get dead."*
> Counselllor: "So why do you like that?"
> Child: *"Miss, because me like to see dead people. Me like to touch de dead people dem"*

In 30% of the cases investigated, the children had been personally exposed to multiple types of traumatic incidents involving gun warfare, child abuse and/or physical injury due to traffic accidents..

Given the nature of the trauma that the children experienced, the writer and two separate independent experts[37] determined that, in assessing these children for trauma using the traditional behavioural definitions found in the Diagnostic Statistical Manual for Mental Disorders, it was surprising that only a small proportion of the sample interviewed, exhibited concrete symptoms of Post-Traumatic Stress Disorder or other disorders usually associated with exposure to trauma at the level experienced by these children. It could be concluded therefore, that there was (a) some evidence of resilience being exhibited by these children, and/or (b) that they were exhibiting

---

37 Drs. Joan Lesser and Marjorie Cooper, Smith College, School of Social Workers, Massachusetts, USA, in a visit to the UWI Violence Prevention clinic in 2004.

uncharacteristic symptoms that hitherfore had not been documented by mental health clinicians as symptomatic of Post-Traumatic Stress disorder, or (c) they were exhibiting a traditional disease, e.g., depression, but their symptoms were being manifested in a different form. This writer suggests that both of these variables must be taken into consideration in evaluating the effects of violence on Jamaican children. The model overleaf describes some possible typologies that could explain the children's reactions and suggests that the term, the "Ah Nuh Nutten" syndrome, could be a form of depression that some of the children are experiencing as an adjustment reaction.

Trauma Assessment Instrument for the Caribbean Child (TAICC)

In an effort to assess the level of trauma found in Jamaican children, the writer sought to produce the prototype of a Trauma Assessment Instrument for the Caribbean Child (TAICC) which made use of the empirical data and predictive models developed by the writer and discussed in chapter two. It is anticipated that this Trauma Assessment Instrument could possibly be used in the Caribbean to determine levels of trauma in children for the purpose of effective intervention after the appropriate reliability and validity tests have been completed (Figure 18).

The Trauma Assessment Instrument uses a mathematical model similar to the eco-scan technique used to evaluate the ecological framework of clients in a psycho-social context (NASW 2001), and was done by the writer in conjunction with graduate students from the University of the West Indies (UWI) Department of Sociology, Psychology and Social Work.[38]

The TAICC (Fig. 18) is a three-page document, which is computer-based, but can also be used in a pencil and paper format. The first section of the TAICC, the Client Profile, gives basic information on the child and the presenting problem/crisis, using a numerical scale. The second section of the TAICC assesses The Nature of the Trauma, also using a numerical scale. The variables include, for example, the number of traumatic episodes the child encountered. The third section of the TAICC assesses the Support Structure of the child and scores the child/client based on issues such as the presence or absence of parents, their migration status, as well as other environmental factors,

---

38 The students involved in the conceptualization of the Trauma Assessment Instrument – D'Oyen Williams, Patrice Samuels and Patricia Prescott. (2004).

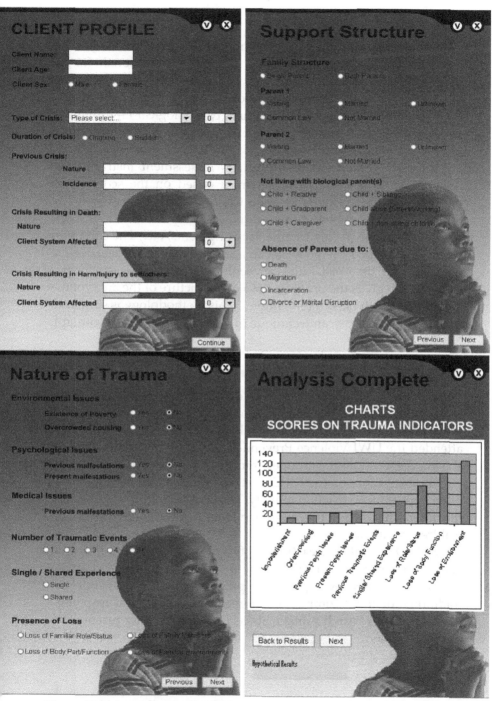

Figure 18: Trauma Assessment Instrument for the Caribbean Child (TAICC) – a computer-based assessment instrument developed by the author

such as overcrowding in their living condition, which may affect the child's psychological and social situation. The rationale for the development of this instrument is based upon the fact that children in the Caribbean who experience violence and trauma have to deal with variables within their social and psychological environment, which are often not found in the societies from which the traditional assessment instruments emanate.

The fourth dimension of the trauma assessment instrument is represented as a cumulative statement based on the scores from pages 1, 2 and 3 and therefore seeks to summarize the coping ability of the client by combining the positives (family and other support) with the negative (recent trauma, lack of parents, etc.) The computer version developed by the writer in association with students of the University of the West Indies presents this as a histogram or bar graph which gives the professional a quick picture of the areas of the child's life which need intervention[39]. This methodology is similar to that used in the eco-scan technique (a graphic form of the eco-map). NASW 1998[40]

The Overall Impact of Violence on Children

The model overleaf summarizes the differential impact that ongoing violence and trauma has had on children in Jamaica. This was based on documentation by this writer, on children affected by violence who attended the UWI Violence Prevention Clinic from 1996 to 2004. As shown, the reactions are grouped into two main categories: (A) Overt Observable Reactions and (B) Covert Non-Observable Reactions that often appear as no reaction initially. The chart therefore summarizes the differential impact that ongoing violence and trauma has had on children in Jamaica.

Overt Observable Reactions refer to reactive emotional and behavioural responses exhibited by a child or adolescent that can be seen over time by a parent or professional. These include the traditional or more common emotional and behavioural responses associated with Post-Traumatic Stress Disorder or other reactions to trauma such as

---

39 D'oyen Williams, M.Sc., Patrice Samuels, MSW, Patricia Prescott M.Sc

40 The eco-scan is a computerized assessment tool based on the principles of the eco-map. The use of this technique was documented in a publication from the National Association of Social Workers in 1998.

Chart 7: *Impact of violence and trauma on children/youth*

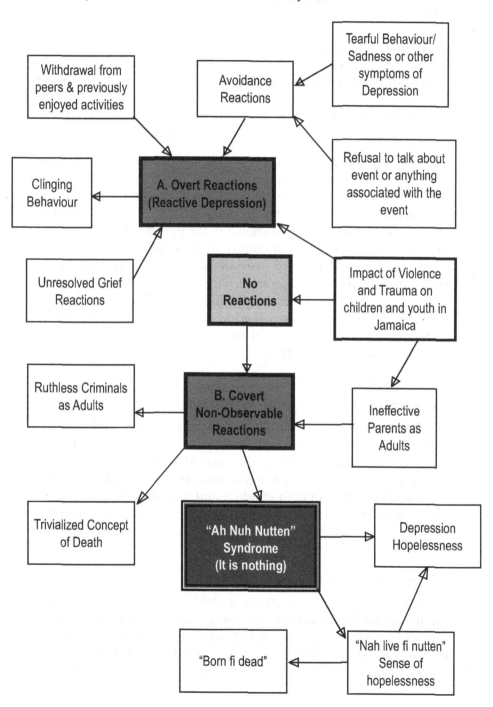

- Aggressive Reactions, e.g. excessive fighting (verbal or physical), bullying and extortion, oppositional defiant disorder, and conduct disorder.
- Withdrawal Reactions, e.g. isolation from peers.
- Development of phobias and fears associated, for example, with early death, fear of the outdoors, fear of the night and being outside.
- Avoidance Reactions, e.g., clinging behaviours, school refusal, truancy, lack of involvement in activities previously enjoyed.

Covert Non-Observable Reactions are another group of reactions that are of great concern to the author. Though they may present as no reaction, they have both **long-term** and **short-term** effects and are caused by the children being over-exposed to violence in their families and communities. As shown in the model, one of the results of these children living in a culture of violence is that they often have overwhelmed parents who are unable to adequately fulfill their parenting roles. Some of these parents displace their feelings of inadequacy onto their children by abusing them in some cases, and neglecting them in other cases. It is important to note that when these children become adults many of them repeat the cycle and become ineffective parents themselves.

Long-term reactions

Ineffectiveness as parents - cycle of violence

As shown in the model, children exposed to trauma and violence may show no observable reactions as children in the short term, but in the long term, in adulthood, they may show a variety of psychological reactions, which may make them ineffective parents. They may be detached from their children and may become disengaged, resulting in ineffective supervision, and the children may develop a range of emotional and behavioural problems, thus repeating the cycle of violence.

Ruthlessness/ lack of reverence for childhood

The other long-term issue affecting children who experience such trauma is that, if they do in fact become criminals, they show a level of ruthlessness, which is based in their own childhood experiences of over exposure to death and violence (sexual as well as community violence). These children also exhibit a sense of detachment and apathy as it relates to the effects of violence on the emotions, which they learn through the socialization experience from family and community members. There is also a lack of reverence for childhood as a special and precious stage of human development. These are the criminals who are able to kill children.

O N E ten year-old boy who had witnessed sexual violence committed against his infant sister and multiple cases of community shootings, some in his own household, was particularly nonchalant about rape and other violent acts against women. In a focus group session at the UWI violence prevention programme with other ten and eleven year-old boys who were witnesses of violence, this child stated that he could envision killing a woman who was unfaithful to him. Other boys in the group seemed to think that because these acts of abuse went unpunished, it made it acceptable for a man to either abuse or kill a girl or a woman.

Short-term reactions

The short-term effect of trauma include a disturbing trend referred to by this author as the **Ah nuh Nutten [It is nothing] Syndrome**: This refers to the extent to which children who have been traumatized have developed an ego defence mechanism of apathy to try to numb the pain they feel. If this defence mechanism is overused, or if it is undetected, or if there is no intervention to address their needs, the child or adolescent may develop a sense of hopelessness, as exemplified by some urban based gangs who name themselves the "**born fi dead posse**" or the "**nah live fi nutten crew**". This leads to a generation of youth who have a trivialized concept of death and dying. Those who show criminal tendencies in adolescence and young adulthood therefore refer to the act of killing as "making a duppy [ghost]". Again trivializing the concept of death, showing no reverence for life or for he sanctity of human life

O N E fifteen-year-old who murdered a fourteen year old in one urban school had threatened to *"mek a duppy"* prior to graduating. Having committed the murder of his schoolmate, he told a shocked group of his schoolmates *"ah tell yuh ah was gwine mek a duppy before ah leave school."* This represents a trivialized concept of death and dying, which is dangerous for our youth. This particular child had been socialized by criminals in his community as his parents had abdicated all parental responsibility through migration in one instance and through incarceration for most of his life. This child described his father as a *"retired don."* This meant, he explained, that his father *"used to give orders but now him tek orders from a younger man."*

Behavioural indicators

It is important to note that the impact of violence on children and families will have different manifestations depending on the symptoms and/or the behaviours presented by the child. The different types of problems shown are presented as part of a wide range of behavioural definitions. The children's emotional and behavioural problems may manifest themselves as a range of behaviours, which include:

(a)   Anti-social behaviour
(b)   Conduct disorder behaviour
(c)   Depression reaction
(d)   Anger Control/Management problems
(e)   Problems related to emotional distress
(f)   Problems related to lack of self-esteem/self-worth.

The symptoms presented by children with behavioural problems include lying, stealing, lack of remorse, disruptive behaviours, frequent fighting, hyper-activity, inattentiveness and other disruptive behaviour whereas the symptoms presented by children with emotional problems include phobias, sleeping and eating problems, suicidal ideation and other symptoms of depression such as prolonged sadness and frequent crying, withdrawal from peers, and reduction of involvement in previously-enjoyed activities.

The 'Ah Nuh Nutten' [it is nothing] Syndrome: protective scar tissue

One of the most interesting behavioural reactions is the ah nuh nutten syndrome (described earlier in the text). The model suggests that, as mentioned earlier in this chapter, there are specific adaptive (or maladaptive) responses that the children have developed as coping mechanisms which require further investigation. In investigating the "Ah Nuh Nutten Syndrome", the researcher used the model above (Chart 7) to explain the range of reactions that are displayed by Jamaican children and adolescents as a result of the various forms of violence they experience and see the "Ah Nuh Nutten Syndrome" as part of a range of maladaptive response to the stress of living with ongoing violence. As observed earlier, this is similar to reactions seen by children living in war-torn countries such as Afghanistan and Africa.[41]

A form of reactive depression

Another issue illustrated by the model suggests that the non-observable reactions of the children include, but are not confined to, forms of reactive depression which are similar to those which gave rise to various names previously assigned to inner-city urban Jamaican gangs, such as the "Nah Live Fi Nutten Crew", which links back to older names which emerged out of the 1970s such as the "Born Fi Dead Posse". The findings suggest that if these children continue to grow up without intervention, the society may be producing a set of children, youth and then adults who are at risk of developing, or have already developed, a pervasive sense of hopelessness and an almost trivialized sense of death and dying.

Summary

The central thesis of this text, therefore, is that the depressive reactions presented by the children and adolescents in the Jamaica context, manifest themselves by way of several additional symptoms which are not presented in the traditional literature as symptoms of depression. These symptoms such as the "Ah Nuh Nutten Syndrome" and statements such as "born fi dead" and "nah live fi nutten" statements are defense mechanisms rather than displays of bravado developed by Jamaican children to cope with inordinately high levels of violence

---

41 Children of Islam, CNN, Atlanta, Georgia, USA.

and trauma. These defense mechanisms act as a type of "scar tissue" to protect the children's minds from bearing the brunt of the trauma and violence they have to face on an ongoing basis.

The action of the perpetrators represents what could be termed a pathological shift in levels of social apathy. This is expressed in a shift in the pattern of crime that has been taking place gradually over the past decade. The entire society has, however, sat on the sidelines for years, watching speechless and numbed as our urban terrorists strike again and again at the heart of civil society by harming child after child with seeming abandon. A pattern of criminal behaviour where the most vulnerable members of a society are slaughtered like animals is as much the responsibility of the perpetrators, as it is of the society that has created them.

PRESCRIPTIONS & SOLUTIONS

Caribbean Childhood Under Threat

"Childhood is more than just a space between birth and the attainment of adulthood. It is more than just the time before a person is considered an adult."

Childhood under threat – UNICEF (State of the World's Children, 2005)

T H E term "childhood" implies a separate and safe space which must be conceived of as being delineated and apart from the space that is set aside for adulthood.

Every country of the world strives to ensure that the years of childhood are of special significance, where children are healthy and can be protected from harm. In every society, no matter how poor or under-resourced, children are expected to live in environments surrounded by supportive and living adults who work collectively at the level of the family, community and society to ensure that children can grow and develop to their full potential, and where every child can be treated as a special and precious human being.

The information presented in this book sounds a resounding warning that leaves one with the impression that "childhood" as previous generations have known it in Jamaican society, is in fact under threat. Increasingly, as the data and statements from the children in this book show, violence is taking away from them every semblance of security in their homes and family lives. Conflict and violence continue to cause the deaths of their parents and close family members.

Photo 6: Children from a high school in Kingston, Jamaica, participating in the "Behaviour Hype Zone" a programme developed by the author to reinforce positive behaviour in youth

As small island developing states of the Caribbean Basin become caught up in the rapid escalation of the use of technology and the accompanying effects of globalization in almost every facet of daily life, they have become affected by the phenomena. These states have become increasingly vulnerable to a range of social problems which are impacting negatively on their nation's children in a variety of ways – violence against them and involving them being one of the issues of most concern.

Violence Against Children: A Betrayal of Trust

Violence causes in our children a betrayal of the trust and a betrayal of the sense of hope that they need to have as an important part of their psycho-social development. As discussed earlier in this book, at the level of the community, the mezzo level, the Jamaican society shows an increasing tendency for the blurring of the lines between what is acceptable versus unacceptable in dress, music, speech or behaviour for a child. This has led to a scenario where children are losing their lives, simply because they are children and are particularly vulnerable on all fronts. As one writer described them, they have increasingly become "soft targets" for a variety of predators in the societies from which they come. Children, regardless of their gender, have continued to be targets for sexual predators. Other children are preyed upon by a variety of criminals in their communities who see them as easy prey for a variety of criminal acts. Jamaican society, for example, espouses a culture where the music, the cultural practices, traditions and norms which have acted as protectors for our children for decades, even centuries, are no longer working to protect them. These time-worn ethical and cultural norms and values have been the foundation of child rearing practices which our forefathers preached for centuries. These practices have held together the social fabric of our society since its inception. This social fabric is in danger of disintegrating if we fail to understand the serious changes and shifts in the patterns of childhood socialization, which focus so much on violence as a part of our children's daily lives, in fact, their very existence. The society desperately needs comprehensive and holistic solutions and these solutions need to be implemented sooner rather than later.

Solutions Must Be Comprehensive and Multi-dimensional

The discussion in the previous chapters has shown that the problem of violence against children and families in Jamaica is a complex one needing comprehensive solutions. This chapter will therefore look at some of these solutions in terms of the social policies and interventions that need to be implemented at the level of the community. All of these interventions must work concomitantly so that all services are integrated and interrelated.

Policies to protect our children from violence cannot be implemented in a piecemeal and an ad hoc manner. Quick and urgent action need to be put in place at all levels of the society, to prevent and reduce the present scourge of violence affecting Jamaica's children and their families. These policies must be presented within the context of the findings and analyses of the original research originating from the country and the children, youth, and the families concerned.

The rationale for these policies and interventions is based on the notion that solutions at the macro level (which refers to actions of the State) also sets the tone for values and attitudes at the mezzo community level, which in turn results in programmes or the lack of programmes to meet the needs of children in an age-appropriate way. Values at the community level in turn influence the responses of parents in terms of the degree to which they see the importance of protecting their children.

Preconditions for social policies

The social policy prescriptions and solutions presented in this section, and detailed in the rest of this chapter, are based on three basic preconditions.

The first one is that **all childhood including those of the children of the Caribbean, must continue to be seen as a "special place" where each and every child can have a chance to grow and to their full potential."** The second precondition is that, regardless of the society in which a child spends his/her childhood, "children are seen to possess the unique capacity to respond positively to appropriate care and treatment, even more so than adults." (Children's Defense Fund 1976).

This means that it is very **important for policy makers and social practitioners to emphasize the value of rehabilitative, therapeutic, as well as preventive services for children and youth,** particularly those who are risk for violence, whether as victims or perpetrators.

The third major precondition is based on the fact that there must be **reduced levels of crime and violence in the broader society** in order for a reduction to take place at the individual level. Law and order at the broader societal level will therefore create a safer environment for children and their families at the level of the individual and family. The Task Force Report on Crime and Violence which was commissioned by the Government of Jamaica in 2004 set out in detail the prescriptions for the management of crime and violence at the various levels of the society. These prescriptions were documented as solutions to curb and reduce the incidence of criminal behaviour generally. The broad components of these recommendations include short-term and long-term policy provisions. The major recommendations from this Task Force are presented below with a discussion on how these policies could be implemented so as to reduce the impact of crime and violence on children, in particular:

"The need to rebuild the moral authority of elected officials who must lead the fight against crime and violence". This recommendation presupposes a political climate where political leaders need to take the moral high ground as part of a campaign to institute a zero tolerance for accommodating violence from the top down. The recommendation suggests encouraging politicians to disassociate themselves from those members of the society who may be associated with violence, and generally supporting and endorsing non-violence in the society.

Policing and legislative provisions to deal with hard-core criminals. This would require the use of the full power and authority of the State to ensure effective law enforcement. It also refers to the use of a variety of policing techniques including community policing, which has been touted as one of the most effective policing techniques for dealing with the annihilation of gangs, and general violence reduction/prevention at the level of the community, through improved intelligence gathering techniques (This model was used by a US-based agency, PERF, a community policing project implemented in the Grants Pen area of Kingston in the mid-nineties.)

Providing community-based initiatives designed to give individuals and communities the opportunity to "redeem themselves" and/or to become rehabilitated. This should include initiatives such as restorative justice programmes where victims and perpetrators are given an opportunity to interact in a supervised environment, usually within the confines of a penal institution or a social service programme. This could be started with juveniles within correctional institutions, and would help young perpetrators to be held accountable for their actions and also prevent the distancing from their victims as portrayed in the narrative described earlier in this book. Such a programme could be integrated into a model of restorative justice as practised in the state of Oregon in the United States where perpetrators at the community level interface with their victims.

Other macro policy recommendations

In addition to the Jamaican Task Force Report on Crime and Violence, several international conferences and various think tanks have been held locally and regionally on the issue of violence affecting children in the Caribbean. One important meeting was a regional consultation referred to as "The Caribbean Consultation on Violence against Children" held in Port-of-Spain, Trinidad and Tobago, in March 2005, under the auspices of a number of regional agencies in collaboration with UNICEF. The report from this consultation was part of the UN Secretary General's Assessment of Violence against Children in the **Caribbean** Region 2006. In this report the broad findings suggested that the impact of the violence affecting children was differentially applied throughout the Caribbean with the most serious being felt in Jamaica and Trinidad and Tobago. The major recommendations coming from that report spoke to four areas of inadequacy relating to children and violence. These were grouped into six main areas:

1.   **Inadequacies in the legal framework, policies and procedures relating to the protection of children from violence.** This issue was also one of those reiterated by the Task Force set up in Jamaica in 2002 to look at crime and violence. This is also an issue which was highlighted by the US State Department as needing attention as it related to the prosecution of those individuals in Jamaica who may be involved in the intra-island trafficking of children. Though the research pointed to the possible compliance of adolescents in particular, and their parents, the issue of the inability of the State to adequately prosecute these individuals could be viewed as being directly related to the inadequacies in the legal framework surrounding the protection of children generally. The above report, however, broadened the recommendation relating to legal policies and included :

   • **public education programmes** to sensitize the public on laws relating to the treatment of children, and

   • **training of professionals in the law enforcement system.** One could add, however, the need to train professionals in the juvenile justice system including judges and attorneys who work with the family courts, regarding alternative sentencing strategies for dealing with young offenders who are among the perpetrators of violence against young children. Elsewhere, the report emphasizes the need to introduce rehabilitative programmes involving community service into the menu of options for children in the juvenile justice system.

2.   **Inadequacies relating to services for children experiencing violence in their homes.** Some of the recommendations from the UN Secretary General's Report, which were not previously mentioned by other reports in this area included:

   • **The need for family support systems** to help and encourage families to bond and connect with their children. The report also emphasized the importance of supporting fathers and fathering. This could be done through a network of Family Enrichment Centres attached to existing service delivery systems for families, using intervention models where parents can be given the opportunity in individual family settings or group or community settings to understand how to work with children who pose specific challenges to their parents.

- **Mandatory child abuse reporting.** They reported that Jamaica was the only State in the Caribbean which had moved legislatively to implement mandatory reporting. It is important to note, however, that this important legal initiative could become ineffectual, even in Jamaica, if the necessary resources are not in place for intensive public education, so that parents actually report the problem. It is important to note also that some agencies working with child abuse suggest that it is possible that some forms of abuse have become so normalized in some communities that the anticipated increase that one would expect with mandatory reporting is not yet taking place in Jamaica −several years after the legislation was put into place.

- **Preventing and reducing anti-social behaviour in children** was reiterated in this report as essential to preventing violence in later adolescence and adulthood. The importance of targetting parents, teachers and community stakeholders for training in non-violent methods of conflict resolution and problem solving was again highlighted.

3. **Inadequacies in policies to protect children experiencing violence in communities and on the streets.** Monitoring of level of exposure of children to all forms of violence as witnesses and consumers of violence, e.g. music and other media

    Some of the recommendations in this area must include the use of the media to challenge cultural and social norms which are harmful to children at the community level. As the children of Jamaica and the Caribbean gyrate to music which speaks to revenge and violence as methods of resolving conflict, many adults seem oblivious to the harm this does to children who are at risk as victims and as perpetrators or potential perpetrators .The use of national broadcasting monitoring agencies to safeguard the interest of children must be seen as an important component of any policy to protect children from violence at the community level

4. **Inadequacies in providing services to children who are at risk for violence in Schools.**-Intra-curricular and after-school

programmes for assessment and intervention with children at risk for violence.

- Schools must be equipped with a range of intervention programmes within the guidance counselling curriculum as well as within the ambit of after-school programming to assess, detect and intervene with children who are determined to be at risk for violence within the school, home or community. Examples of specific programmes are included in Appendix IX as part of a "user-friendly" matrix of solutions referred to as "A Blueprint for Action - Managing violence in Schools" designed so that they can be copied by guidance counsellors, social workers and other professionals for use in the school systems. This report, among other recommendations, expressed the need to undergird these programmes with an element of spirituality — the possibility of strengthening the existing strong spiritual base within our schools and communities which exists in most Caribbean territories which are not hamstrung by constitutional clauses that would prevent this.

5. **Inadequacies in provision of services to protect children from violence in institutions: Need for core performance indicators.** Ongoing systems for the careful selection and training of child care workers in child care and correctional institutions is a basic prerequisite for any modern child welfare system which uses institutionalization as a mechanism for the care and protection of children (Crawford-Brown 1999). This would mean that existing systems of child welfare which employ this mechanism should consider reforming/mapping the current hiring procedure for human resource personnel working in its existing children's homes and correctional institutions, The use of core performance indicators for these staffers could be linked to in-service training to better serve the needs of children in their care.

- Strengthening family support programmes through reform in the child care and juvenile justice systems. This would reinforce the importance of family reunification - an important component of any modern/contemporary child welfare system (Crawford-Brown 1999), and the revamping of current adoption and foster care programmes to make them more efficient and effective as an alterative to the institutionalization of children (Crawford-Brown 2000).

- Legislative reform in this area was also emphasized particularly in the area of juvenile justice where the institution of restorative justice as a strategy of rehabilitation for young perpetrators was noted.

6. **Inadequacies in service provision to deal with violence against children who work.** The report emphasized the need to provide alternative educational opportunities for children who were working on the street. It is to be noted that the report emphasized the importance of Parenting Education, Public Education, as well as the importance of Data Collection and Research for each of the areas in this report. It is important to note that these three initiatives could be addressed meaningfully through the use of technology (see Appendix VI: Caribbean Child Welfare Network).

Violence Against Children: A Complex Problem Needing Comprehensive Solutions

As shown by the issues discussed above, the problems and the solutions proposed that have been presented by the various task forces and conferences held to discuss this matter of violence against children are many and varied, and so the strategies and interventions used must reflect this. It is to be noted that the solutions to these problems sometimes fall outside of the traditional medical models of therapeutic interventions normally used for dealing with emotional and psychological problems. The interventions that follow, therefore, have been used in a variety of agencies throughout the Caribbean to reduce the problems relating to violence, and are presented to give Caribbean practitioners a wide range of options in dealing with the different problems which occur in the different contexts. The social problems and their solutions are therefore organized in relation to the differential levels of intervention within which they can be implemented. They are presented as follows: Macro Level (Societal) Interventions, Mezzo Level (Community) Interventions, and Micro Level (Individual) Interventions.

Interventions that work: best practice models – International and regional

Oregon Model

There are a number of contemporary strategies used to deal with crime and violence in urban areas. In a recent *Time Magazine* article (March 26, 2007) on crime mapping in Oregon, the report cited Violence Prevention involving prevention as an important method used by the state to combat crime, similar to the multi-modal treatment methods used by the UWI. The article cited a social programme in Oregon which used a strategy of intervention with perpetrators as well as victims. This programme, which targeted children at risk from violence-prone communities, involved engaging them in after-school, community-based initiatives involving reparation and restorative justice programmes, as well as a range of other multi-modal therapies.

Unitas Model

Another successful community-based programme coming out of the Bronx (Eismann 2000) uses a similar programme of adolescent mentorship and engagement to provide "street therapy" for children needing alternative parenting, to significantly decrease crime rates in one borough of the Bronx over a thirty-year period. These interventions were adapted and redesigned to address the unique problems of Caribbean children, and have been tested with children in the Caribbean through the UWI Violence Prevention Programme.

"Get on Board" (Barbados) Model:
Psycho-educational intervention for parents and children

In Barbados, one such programme initiated by the Department of Corrections for children at risk for violence and other behaviour problems used a tourist ship that was in harbour to run a similar programme for at risk adolescents and their parents. This programme, dubbed *"Get on Board Barbados"*, was an innovative programme to use the resources of the tourist industry to provide counselling to families for children at risk for violence. As part of that programme, parents would attend for parenting classes on deck while their children were engaged in group counselling and other psycho-educational activities below deck.

The novelty of using a ship was so attractive that there was maximum attendance and participation, and at the end of the project, children and parents were treated to a trip on the ocean.

Photo 7: "Get on board Nautical Programme" used off-duty tourist boats to host social intervention programmes for parents and children at risk for behavioural problems

Mandatory play spaces for children: the Pocket Park Model

This is an initiative that follows closely on the above model as it assumes that child-friendly communities will enact mandatory building codes which include the designation of simple geographical areas that have to be set aside as play spaces for children. This could be set up by urban planning agencies such as the National Housing Authorities and could then be established with more or less play equipment, depending on available funding. Such spaces should be established in every community or housing scheme constructed in Jamaica. This is reminiscent of a policy initiative set up by the Michael Manley administration in the 1970s, adapted from Cuba and implemented by Jamaica's then First Lady Beverly Manley. This initiative could be revisited, as it is a model which could be built on our rich oral history and provide a space where community plays and performing arts initiatives are carried out such as now occurs in Allman Town and other community-based, child-friendly community arenas.

Communities with safe spaces for play for children could decrease the extent to which later adolescents become perpetrators of violence against small children, as programmes involving children and adolescents such as those described above would have safe places where they could interact under the supervision of adults.

The solutions discussed above are many and varied. It is useful, however, to note that, given the range of possible interventions and activities that exist for working with children who had experienced violent trauma or children who are perpetrators of violence, in order to determine an intervention plan for Jamaica, a basic intervention philosophy should undergird all interventions. This intervention philosophy is presented in the form of a clinical community-based intervention model for children affected by violence and trauma, developed by the author and used in the UWI Violence Prevention Programme for the past thirteen years. It is referred to as The Multi-modal Nurturant Model of Community Care and is designed for the Caribbean, where there is a dearth of such models documented.

Interventions That Work: Local Model
Multi-Modal Nurturant Model of Community Care

The multi-modal interventions discussed and presented in this section lay the foundation for the policies and prescriptions implemented by the UWI Violence Prevention Programme which operates as an outreach project of the Department of Sociology, Psychology and Social Work. This project is part of the Department's Centre for Population, Community and Social Change.

The Violence Prevention Programme was established by the author in 1996 as a family clinic. It is seen as a laboratory for the development of clinical social work as well as community practice. The main objective of the programme is to prevent/reduce violence in the general society by intervening with children and their families who are affected by violence in its different forms. This includes community violence, interpersonal violence and various forms of institutionalised violence. The programme offers a clinic for children and families who are victims and perpetrators of violence and also

Photo 8: The UWI Violence Prevention Programme

provides Training, Research, and Advocacy services. Other objectives include:

I   Provide direct and effective intervention at the micro level, to children through a campus-based social service agency, run by faculty and students of a tertiary level institution.

II   Provide intervention at the community (mezzo) level to professionals in the school system, social workers, as well as other community professionals and paraprofessionals.

III   Provide learning opportunities for students at the tertiary level where they can develop and practise innovative strategies for addressing the problem of children and families affected by violence in all its forms.

Since the programme started it has provided direct clinical services to over 1,000 children and their families who have visited the agency through referrals from the school system, churches, as well as those who have participated in weekend camps and summer camps in Jamaica (2004) and Trinidad and Tobago (2005). All of these children were exposed to violence in their homes, schools, and communities.

Through this programme the author has developed and produced a series of Assessment, Counselling and Training materials (ACT NOW) for Caribbean professionals working with children exposed to violence (see Appendix VII). Using these training materials, numerous workshops and seminars have been conducted throughout the Caribbean mainly in Jamaica, Cayman Islands, and Trinidad and Tobago. These workshops have trained over 500 professionals in educational and social service systems in these countries on various aspects of violence prevention, crisis management, and anger management and conflict resolution.

Therapeutic team

The model chosen for the process of working with children traumatized by violence, needing specialized intervention is one of community care using specially trained care-givers who replicate the family in terms of the inter-generational, and inter-disciplinary nature of the clinical team. These care-givers were chosen on the basis of the extent to which they represented a range of individuals of various age groups in their communities to whom the children could go for help and assistance. Therapists were referred to as ithe team provided a range of non-clinical but supportive services, such as feeding the children, playing group games such as football as well as spiritual counselling. This model is an experimental one that has been used at the UWI Violence Prevention Programme for fourteen years, and has been used with children and their families who are victims of violence as well as perpetrators.

The composition of the team was deliberately structured using a mixed demographic profile of persons which included a middle-aged male Rastafarian and a retired basic school teacher as paraprofessionals who work alongside graduates of the University with backgrounds in guidance counselling and community development. The overall programme was developed and is supervised by a full-time faculty member who is a trained clinical social worker, with post-doctorial training in family therapy, grief therapy, and play therapy. The supervision of students is bolstered by the services of an interdisciplinary advisory committee of persons who represent a range of allied disciplines such as child development, psychiatry, clinical psychology, and community development. Referrals are made when necessary to relevant social service agencies. The multi-modal interventions discussed and presented in this chapter lay the foundation for the policies and prescriptions implemented and recommended. These interventions were developed and tested on a foundation of empirical research (Crawford-Brown 2007).

Councelling staff structure: therapeutic camps

The counselling staff is therefore structured to provide services at three levels:

A. Peer/Junior Counsellors. Highly educated and motivated youngsters from the same communities as clients who were seen as role models by these clients. These youngsters lived in and around the communities where the children reside.

B. Senior Counsellors. Highly trained and experienced clinic social workers who were trained at the Master's level. This group was supplemented by a group of:

C. Community Para-professionals. Members of this group were hand-picked to provide a high quality of community care such as provision of meals, supervision of artwork, documentation and registration procedures, bathroom breaks as well as general supervision during the therapeutic process. Many of these para-professionals also assisted with prayer activities which were an integral part of the therapeutic process. Participative prayers were held at the beginning and end of each therapeutic session. The junior counsellors and paraprofessionals were trained in basic child development and were able to refer clients to senior counsellors when necessary.

The community care model includes the use of hug/attachment therapy, using gentle but firm discipline through structured individual and group intervention.

Therapeutic interventions used

The interventions used by the UWI Violence Prevention Programme involves the use of traditional clinical intervention techniques such as play therapy, the use of a Healing Garden, small and large group counselling sessions, mentorship (peer and police) psycho-drama, puppetry and psycho-educational intervention. These intervention techniques have mainly been used with children and adolescents, whereas community-based interventions involving focus groups, and community group work have been used with parents, mentors and community members. These activities were therapeutic and were designed and tested to interface with children and their families at risk, at different levels of interventions, namely the individual level as well as at the level of the community and small groups. These interventions will now be described in some detail.

Play therapy: The emergence of a Caribbean model

Play therapy is one of the most effective intervention modalities for working with traumatized children, regardless of the source of their trauma. "Play is to children as work is to adults", thus play therapy is a very effective way of entering into a child's world (Chetnik 1989). This modality however, has not been widely used in the Caribbean, and many clinical social work and psychology practitioners who may have learnt this technique at the tertiary level, seem to have abandoned the modality and have not pursued postgraduate training in this very important area. The result is that play therapy in the Caribbean has historically been shrouded in "mysticism" and has therefore been underutilized in the region. Given the reality that children in the Caribbean have so much creativity in the fields of art and music, and given the fact that dance seems to be "built into their DNA", this is regrettable. It is this creativity that the author has sought to harness in developing a Caribbean model of play therapy which uses unique aspects of Caribbean culture in therapeutic play wit children. A variety of play therapy methods are used in this intervention model. They include, Art therapy, Sand play (wet and dry), Puppetry using Psycho-drama and role play, as well as family sculpting and enactment.

Family sculpting for children. The use of Sculpting using Caribbean dolls and animal figures is also utilized. In this model sculpting involves the use of complete doll families or animal families which are manipulated by the child to show how a particular family member interacts with others.

Puppetry. This method is extensively utilized to help children to express and process their feelings about violence ad other issues. The older children and adolescents also use puppetry as a method of psycho-educational intervention .to do role play showing incidents of violence in their schools and communities as well as alternative ways of resolving conflicts.

Art therapy (painting, drawing, quilts, murals and sculpture): Unresolved grief and other deep-seated emotional issues. In this intervention modality, the children are involved in activities which allow them to purposefully express their feelings about violence through a variety of art forms, namely painting, drawing and sculpture, with clay, play dough or flour dough. The children who are dealing with trauma, unresolved grief, and other bereavement issues also use community murals and quilts done over time by parents and the children themselves. These quilts depict messages to their loved ones and are done with the guidance of adolescent counsellors and adults as part of the therapeutic process.

Psycho-Educational Counseling: Targeted Intervention for Violence Prevention

Anger Management, Conflict Resolution, Bereavement, and Behaviour Change. Children and adolescents in this form of intervention are exposed to a range of psycho-educational activities which included videos, stories and a structured curriculum of information which include posters, workbooks, flash cards, board games and other group games. The objective of these activities is to **develop the emotional intelligence**

Photo 9: Caribbean Social Work students visiting from UWI St Augustine Campus view Puppetry about drug use enacted by inner-city youth at the Wee Cottage on the UWI Mona Campus

of the children and families who were both victims and perpetrators of violence. The psycho-educational activities were developed as a set of Assessment, Counselling and Training packages for Caribbean populations (ACT NOW). These training materials have involved the development and production of four packages consisting of tools and other aids aimed at violence prevention/ and reduction in schools and communities, as follows:

1. Anger management – "Cage that Roaring Rage"
2. Conflict resolution – "Peer Mediation for the Caribbean Adolescent"
3. Ameliorative counselling - "When you need a Hug"
4. Behaviour change for targeted children and adolescents – "The Peace Warriors Programme"

Violence Prevention/Reduction. The counselling tools in package IV were designed as a specific type of violence prevention/reduction intervention known as the *Peace Warrior Programme.* This programme was developed and documented by the author (2003-2005) and involved the development of specific training and intervention tools for Caribbean children which have since been tested with other groups in Jamaica, as well as in Trinidad and Tobago. The methodology of this particular intervention has since been documented (Mattias et al. 2008: 441-445).

Community-Based Counselling for Parents and Children: The Comfort Zone Model

(a) At the community level, through *The Comfort Zone Project*, the children and their parents received counselling and psycho-educational intervention in all matters related to personal, sexual and domestic violence. This programme was based in a police station and the police, who acted as mentors, were involved in the administration of the programme. Adolescent mentors from the community implemented the programme and were "paid" in kind, through a hnot meal, as well as access to the Internet, a yoga programme and material arts classes. These classes were provided by local community members and agencies from the surrounding area.

(b) At the individual level, students and parents received individual and group counselling.

The reality is that, once interventions are done in schools, the moment the children are returned to their communities, there is an absence of direct community intervention with trained professionals who can address their specific needs. Community-based interventions at the community level must be implemented alongside any interventions in the school and the home, as individual therapy.

Integration of Sports/Outdoor Therapy in the Therapeutic Process

Adventure therapy "Let the Children Run". The child-friendly community model would interface well with the *"Let the Children Run"* initiative which is a community-based year-round proposal by the author for children and adolescents ages 5 to 17, where community activities can be sustained to organize year-round track meets for children and youth who want to be involved in athletics, particularly track and field. At present, athletics are confined to those children who are in school. There is a large group of youth who are outside of the traditional school system, that is, children and youth who may be in children's homes or who may have dropped out of school for various reasons, who can make use of the abundance of open green spaces which adorn the Jamaican rural landscape and which can be found in most urban and suburban areas in almost every school in the island.

Given the natural predisposition and ability of Jamaicans in the area of track and field, this initiative is an untapped resource which would have therapeutic benefit particularly for urban youth who often have very few safe places to play and expend their energies. This is a vital component for optimal development of children and youth. In a country like Jamaica with year round excellent weather, this is a model of intervention that could begin with children who are the perpetrators of violence as part of a behaviour modification programme. Outdoor therapy programmes or sports programmes could be integrated into therapeutic activities so that, for example, rewards for involvement in therapy or change in behaviour could be tied to sports-based challenges or activities that use the outdoors as an open theatre for children's creativity. This use of the outdoors may include Healing Gardens for children who have suffered grief loss or trauma, as mentioned below.

Therapeutic Healing Gardens: Grief Counselling

This form of intervention, also using the outdoors was used as a means of grief counselling for cases of unresolved grief. It involved children planting and maintaining a flowering shrub which represented the loss of their loved one. Children were then encouraged to water and maintain their particular plant.

Highway to Heaven: Bereavement Counselling

This is a computer-based strategy used in the UWI Violence Prevention Programme to encourage children to express their feelings towards their loved ones. This strategy which is similar to "the empty chair" technique was found to be very popular with latency aged and pre-adolescents. It is involved writing letters to the deceased significant other telling them about their daily activities and feelings as if they were right there beside them.

Mentorship

Adolescent/Peer Mentorship Model. Mentorship is one of the most effective intervention modalities doe working with children at risk as well as children exposed to violence. (Eismann 1990). These children often need long-term intervention which cannot be addressed using classic therapeutic modalities. Mentorship is a natural community-based resource that is sustainable and is always a valuable method of

Photo 10: Gardening as part of the therapeutic healing process

monitoring and maintaining positive behaviour in children needing behaviour modification or behavior change. It is important to note that adolescent mentors can be good resource personnel for intervention with children at risk, particularly at the community level. The UWI Violence Prevention Programme developed a project in mentorship with adolescents trained in child development. They were mentors for younger latency-aged girls and boys who were at risk for behav-

Photo 11: Here, a group of peer adolescents learn how to use the 'Island Game'. Adolescents trained in the use of Adventure Therapy assisted with young campers at risk

ioural problems. They provided mentorship services in exchange for yoga, and martial arts for their own personal development.

When these programmes are implemented under the guidance of adolescents who are positive role models, it provides sustainability and a form of community service for the more privileged youths in the community and society. This model presupposes a child-friendly environment as it is based on the maximum participation of older adolescents and youth from a community that is focused on its children.

Police Mentorship Model. One community–based project with which the UWI Violence Prevention Programme was involved was the use of Police as mentors for the children and adolescents at risk. Training for these mentors in child development was however a pre-requisite for this mentorship programme. The programme had limited success as trained police were often transferred out of the targeted communities and there was little commitment by the Police establishment to the project thought it was funded heavily by international donors. The

Photo 12: Police and mentors in the Police Mentorship Programme

basic concept is however easily replicable, worked successfully in the project period to reduce instances of adolescents going into gangs and crime (Crawford-Brown 2004) and is worth using as a model of intervention with youngsters at risk for violence.

Peer mediation: "The Peace Warrior Programme". With the assistance of Dr. Beverly McKenzie, retired educator, the author developed package II, a school/community-based intervention programme, using the well-documented methodology of Peer Mediation to teach those children and adolescents who are good role models, how to implement a school-wide or a community-based Conflict Resolution programme. This programme is now in place in the Jamaican school system as part of an overall package of Anger Management and other initiatives designed by the Ministry of Education to create safe havens in Jamaican schools (see Appendix VII: Assessment Counselling and Training Packages for Caribbean School - ACT NOW).

Behaviour modification: "The Behaviour Hype Zone"

This is a school-based initiative developed by the author which was tested in one inner-city school in urban Jamaica. It combines the use of peer mediators, dubbed "Peace Warriors", who are selected from each class throughout the school community with a simple behaviour modification system. This programme uses monthly rewards for children who adhere to school rules and simple values, good manners and grooming. These children receive their rewards at these monthly school assemblies where their pictures are taken and displayed as members of the Behaviour Hype Zone for their school. The purpose of this programme is to modify negative behaviours within a particular school by elevating those children with positive behaviours.

Spirituality as a model of intervention

One of the unique features of these various models, is the use of spirituality as an integral part of the various interventions. This involves the use of prayer and meditation as part of an undergirding methodology of the therapeutic programmes. This builds on a culture of strong religiosity, which currently exists in contemporary Jamaican and Caribbean society.

Macro Level Interventions (Long-Term)

These various interventions have to be designed as part of comprehensive violence prevention policies for the home, school and community. The key social policy components of these programmes are as follows:

Target Children at Risk

- Early Warning/Early Detection systems
- Crime Mapping
- Put Social Workers in the educational system
- Ongoing training of school professionals
- Integrated Child Alert Services for missing children
- Re-introduce mandatory school buses[34]
- Web-based data bank of children at risk (include missing and exploited children)
- Development of child welfare resource network of all Agencies and services for children in Jamaica and the Caribbean (www. ccwrn.org)

Provide Ameliorative Services for children and families at risk that are accessible and comprehensive

- Provision of accessible **assessment and intervention services for children** and adolescents with behavioural problems/ Emotional problems.
- Urban/rural poor must be targeted through mobile services
- Effective referral and social service delivery systems

Develop Integrated Systems of Social Service Delivery

- **Link Correctional and Protective/Preventive Child Welfare Services into mainstream educational system.**
- Fill gaps in Service Delivery for latency age and adolescent boys at risk for violence through **alternative schools** (residential)
- Expand skill training and **psycho-educational interventions for girls at risk** for sexual and domestic violence
- Create special "Opportunity" **Day Schools** for At-risk youth

---

34 Socio-educational playgrounds – designated play spaces located principally in schools for use on weekends where children are exposed to curricula outside of the traditional educational system – e.g. music, drama, art and oral history.

Macro Level Intervention (Short-Term)

Child Fatality Legislation

- Establish a database through the office of the Children's Advocate based on Child Fatality legislation which would track the reasons and motives for each case of non-accidental death of each child in Jamaica. Once the motives are determined the relevant agencies with responsibility for preventing child fatality in that area must be given the resources to reduce fatality figures. Each programme must be designed with preventive and intervention components and should be accountable to the Office of the Children's Advocate.

Annual Jamaica House Children's Conference

- Establish annual Jamaica House/prime ministerial conference where all stake holders responsible for maintaining the care and protection and safety of children, are made accountable to the Prime Minister for their areas of expertise. The goal of each agency working together being to reduce the number of child fatalities by a specific time period.

Increase the level of Public Education For Child Protection

- Increase public education and advocacy, by changing the nature of public education on child protection to be "more in your face", e.g. use of billboards (e.g. Photo 5, p. 87), use of pop culture.

Joint sitting of Parliament: annual reports on the status of the Jamaican child

- Establish joint committee of parliament to meet on a regular basis to determine the overall status of the Jamaican Child. This should be the responsibility of the Office of the Children's Advocate and should target the various state agencies such as the Child Development Agency, as well as the international and non-government children's agencies working with children in Jamaica.

Mezzo Level Intervention

Create Child-Friendly Communities

- Socio-educational playgrounds **and mandatory play spaces for** children in all Government housing schemes
- **Re-establishment of school buses** and other protective systems to ensure safe environments for all school children from their homes to school and back.
- Increase numbers of crossing guards at all intersections, using unemployed and trained crossing guards
- Parent Patrols- Set up trained 'parent' patrols in major transportation centres to monitor inappropriate music and conduct on all public transportation. Parent could be trained to offer referrals for children who need special attention
- Establish, monitor and enforce **physical school safety zones for vehicles** for each school including large well-marked speeding zones in front of every school. If necessary these should be monitored by uniformed police or school safety officers with persecutory powers
- Strengthen community-based children and youth homework and activity centres particularly in inner-city and rural communities where children can receive counselling and other academic and social activities when needed. The centres need trained staff who can detect emotional and social problems at the community level and refer families quickly to intervention agencies

Establish after-school community services

- Outreach services to locate girls and boys (8-16 years) who might be at risk as victims and boys who may be conduct-disordered and may need behaviour modification programmes in or out of school

Intervention programmes for perpetrators

- Use crime mapping strategies to determine communities most at risk

Community-based Mentorship Programmes

- Peer/Adolescent and Police Mentorship Programmes

- Parent patrols for transportation sector to monitor lewd music and other inappropriate behaviour in the public transportation sector

Integration of Sports as an integral part of therapeutic process – "Let the Children Run"

- Use sports to heal political and other rifts in garrison and other inner-city communities

Massive Public Education Programme -"Make Childhood Precious Again".

- Include culturally relevant audio-visual and other psycho-educational material on safety in the home, school and on the streets

Photo 13: UWI social work students observe clinical social worker Paulette Gooden process a puppetry session on their perspectives on domestic violence with latency age children from local schools December, 2009

The following section represents the recommendations from this text that could operate at the micro level of intervention. These recommendations could be implemented quickly in the short-term with existing resources.

Micro Level Intervention (Short-Term)

- **Strengthen and expand the capacity of the Child Development Agency** and other children's agencies to provide amelioration of emotional and psychological distress through of play therapy equipment, other counselling tools and aides. Ensure that these services are more available and accessible to the poor and to the neediest children
- **Retool the skills of professionals, e.g. guidance counsellors,** social workers, and aides, children's officers and correctional officers to include the detection of a range of emotional and psychological problems, e.g. depression and post-traumatic disorders in children.
- **Initiate the institution of social workers in the school system,** regionally and locally, to supplement the work of guidance counsellors. These social workers could do the home visits necessary to make adequate assessments of the situation of truant children or habitual late or absent children. This will ensure continuation of care, and could provide the follow-up necessary to prevent children "dropping through the cracks".
- **Infuse school curricula with Violence Management Strategies.** This curriculum content should include a range of violence-related management issues, e.g. anger management, conflict resolution, and emotional intelligence content into the curricula of the primary and high school systems and place this content within the agenda of PTA meetings.

Epilogue

There was a community crisis recently in a central area of urban Kingston, which epitomized attitudes to the concept of prevention, and ultimately attitudes to violence prevention. Like most areas of Kingston there was a large grassy area, covering just under 1 acre, located in the middle of a commercial centre which had caught fire. As a consequence, a bush fire started which spread rapidly. The open arAs the fire spread, vendors and other adults walking alongside the area discussed the fire, wondering out loud whether it would spread further. Individuals spoke on cell phones, others just looked on. Cars slowed down, their drivers looking at the fire, then speeding off again. As the fire engulfed an increasingly large area of grass, a plume of smoke rose into the sky. After 10 minutes, the fire services had still not been called. The driver of a passing car eventually called the emergency services, a fire truck came, and the fire was eventually put out, after scorching a large area of what was once an open green, grassy piece of land.

An analogy can be made here to the attitudes to violence prevention in Jamaica and the Caribbean. Most members of the society and the major stakeholders at the mezzo community level in the system, such as the media, the educational system, the child welfare and correctional systems, schools, NGOs, policy makers, and parents, know the dangers of the escalating levels of violence. However, they bypass the symptoms and root causes of the problem, and focus instead on its manifestations.

Thus the media, for example, spends much of its time and resources focusing on the more sensational aspects of violence affecting children, and spend very little of its resources on careful analysis of the problems, or documenting the solutions in terms of the research, in order to make well-founded social policies and prescriptions based on the empirical evidence.

Conclusion

The task of reducing the incidence of violence against children is one that is daunting, given the scramble for scarce resources in small states such as those which exist in the Caribbean. Violence in these countries are impacted by global, regional and community trends which have seeped insidiously into the psyche of the nation through cultural penetration and the gradual adaptation of a culture of socialization that was the de-mystification of childhood. As we try to extinguish the fires raging around our children, it is imperative that we recognize that we cannot achieve the task in bits and pieces, in isolation. We have to garner the resources of a nation to fight the scourge of violence affecting our children. We must link the fight for our children to the fight against poverty, to the fight against gender imbalances, to the fight for men to regain their place as leaders of our households. We must integrate and retool our services so that the scarce resources stretch further and are more effective. Only with a new thrust focused on integration and collaboration can we begin to take our children out of the fire and out of the line of fire currently being directed at them from myriad places and sources in our society. The important thing is that we must act now, the entire society, to save what is our most precious resource. Failure to act now will be to the peril of the nation and, consequently, to the future of our society as we know it.

REFERENCES

Akers, R. (1964). *Socioeconomic status and delinquent behaviour: A retest*. Journal of Research in Crime and Delinquency, 1, 28-46.

Bahr, S.J. (1979). *Family determinants and effects of deviance*. In W.R. Burr, R. Hill, F.I. Nye, I.L. Reiss (Eds.), Contemporary theories about the family (pp.615-643). New York: Free Press.

Bandura, A.W.M. (1959). **Adolescent Aggression: A Study of the Influence of Child Training Practices and Family Interrelationships**. New York: Ronald Press.

_____. (1973). **Social Learning and Personality Development**. New York: Holt Rinehart and Winston.

_____. (1973). **Aggression: A Social Learning Analysis**. Englewood Cliffs, NJ: Prentice-Hall.

Barland, M., ed. (1976). **Violence in the Family**. Atlantic Highlands, NJ: Humanities Press.

Betse, H., Richardson, (1981). *Developing Life Story Book Programmes for Foster Children*. Child Welfare, Vol. LX, No. 8, New York: Child Welfare League of America.

Blake, J. (1962). **Family structure in Jamaica: The Social Context of Reproduction**. New York: Free Press.

Borely, C.B. (1973). *Adolescence in the Caribbean*. In A. Philips, **Delinquency in Jamaica**. Kingston, Jamaica: Kingston Publishers.

Bowlby, J. (1953). **Child Care and the Growth of Love**. London: Pelican Books.

_____. (1969). **Attachment and Loss, Volume I, Attachment**; London: Hogarth Press.

_____. (1973). **Attachment and Loss, Volume II, Separation Anxiety and Anger**, London: Hogarth Press.

_____. (1980). **Attachment and Loss, Volume III, Loss Sadness and Depression**; London: Hogarth Press.

Brodber, E. (1972). *Abandonment of Children in Jamaica*. Kingston, Jamaica: Institute of Social and Economic Research, University of the West Indies.

Brown, J., Anderson, P., Chevannes, B., (1993). **The Contribution of the Caribbean Man to the Family**. Unpublished Report, Caribbean Child Development Centre, University of the West Indies, Kingston.

Burke, A.W. (1980). *A cross-cultural study of delinquency among West Indian boys*. International Journal of Social Psychiatry, 26(2), 81-87.

Cloward, R.A., & Ohlin, L.G. (1960). **Delinquency and Opportunity**. New York: Free Press.

Child Guidance Clinic. (1989). Unpublished Report for UNICEF on Child Abuse in Jamaica, Kingston.

Coard, P., (1972). *Community Development and Political Patronage*. Institute of Social & Economic Studies, University of the West Indies, Mona.

Cooper, D. (1976). **The Death of the Family**. New York: Penguin Books.

Coser, R.. ed., (1974) **The Family: Its Structures and Functions**. Stony Brook, NY: State University of New York, Family Service Association of America.

Crawford-Brown, C. (1986). *Survey of Services for Children in Jamaica, Survey of Services for Children in the Caribbean*. Kingston, Jamaica: Caribbean Child Development Centre, University of the West Indies, Kingston.

_____. (1987). *An Analysis of the Jamaican Child Welfare System*, Occasional Paper Series No. 1, Kingston, Jamaica: Department of Sociology and Social Work, University of the West Indies.

_____. (1989). *Definitional Framework for Street and Working Children in Jamaica*. Unpublished Report. Department of Sociology, Psychology & Social Work, University of the West Indies (Mona), Kingston.

_____. (1989). *Child Prostitution in Jamaica*. Unpublished Report presented at Conference on Child Prostitution, Stockholm, Sweden.

_____. (1993). *Factors Associated with the Development of Conduct Disorder in Jamaican Male Adolescents*. Doctoral dissertation. New Brunswick, NJ: Rutgers University.

_____. (1998). Evaluation of Debt-swap Agreement between the Netherlands and Jamaica. Report. N.p.

Crawford-Brown, C., Rattray, M.(1994). *The Barrel Children of Jamaica: The Socio-cultural Context of Caribbean Migration*. Unpublished study. Kingston, Jamaica: Department of Sociology and Social Work, University of the West Indies.

_____. (1994). *Working with Caribbean Families*, in Boyd-Webb, N., Ed., Social Work with Multi-Cultural Families. New York: Columbia University Press.

Crawford-Brown, C. (1997). *The Impact of Parent-Child Socialization on the Development of Conduct Disorder in Jamaican Male Adolescents*. In Roopnarine, J.L, and Brown, J., Eds., Caribbean Families: Diversity Among Ethnic Groups, Ablex Publishers, Connecticut.

_____. (1999b). **Who Will Save Our Children: The Plight of the Jamaican Child**. Kingston, Jamaica: Canoe Press, University of the West Indies. Kingston.

_____. (Summer 1999a). *Impact of Parenting on Conduct Disorder in Jamaican Male Adolescents*. **Journal of Adolescence**, Volume

34, No. 134. Libra Publishers, San Diego, California.

_____. (2001). _The Impact of Migration on the Rights of Children & Families in the Caribbean._ In Barrow, C. Ed. **Children's Rights, Caribbean Realities.** Ian Randle Publishers, Kingston, Jamaica.

_____. (2006). _Etiological Framework for Understanding the Development of Criminal Behaviour in Jamaica._ Unpublished Paper presented at the Criminology Conference, Institute of Criminology, University of the West Indies, St. Augustine, Trinidad and Tobago.

_____. (2008). _Issues of Violence in the Caribbean._ In Hickling et al (Eds.) **Caribbean Psychological Perspectives,** CARIMENSA Press, Kingston.

Cumper, G. (1972). _Survey of social legislation in Jamaica._ Kingston, Jamaica: Institute of Social and Economic Research.

D'Alburquerque, K. (1984). _Crime and economic development in the Caribbean._ Journal of Social and Economic Studies (Institute of Social & Economic Research, University of the West Indies), 2, 149-152.

David, G. (1967). _Patterns of Social Functioning in Family Relationships: Natural and Parent-Child Problems._ Toronto: University of Toronto School of Social Work.

Dunn, L. (2002). _Jamaica: Situation of children in prostitution – a rapid assessment._ International Programme on the Elimination of Child Labour. Geneva: International Labour Office.

Economic and Social Survey Jamaica. (1992).

Eldemann, M., Children's Defense Fund, Annual Report, Washington, D.C.

Ellis, H. (1992). **Identifying crime correlates in a developing society: A study of socio-demographic indicators of crime in Jamaican society, 1953-1984.** New York. Peter Lang.

Felker, E. (1975). _Foster-Parenting Young Children: Guidelines from a Foster Parent._ New York: Child Welfare League of America.

Fendrich, M., Warner, V., & Weissman, M.M. (1990). _Family risk factors, parental depression, and psychopathology in offspring._ Developmental Psychology, 26, 232-256.

Fox Harding, L. (1996). **The Family, the State and Social Policy.** London: MacMillan Press.

Friel, L. (1973). _Components of a System of Child Welfare._ Boston, Massachusetts: Committee on Children and Youth.

Frosh, S., Glaser, D. (1988). _Child Sexual Abuse._ London: MacMillan Education.

Gardener, W.T. (1974). **Children with Learning and Behavioural Problems, A Behaviour Management Approach.** Needham Massachusetts: Allyn and Bacon.

Gayle, H., (2004). _A Study of Adolescents in St. Catherine._

Geismar, L.L., & Wood, K.N. (1986). **Families and delinquency: Resocializing the Young Offender.** New York: Human Services Press.

Girvan, N., ed. (1997). **Poverty, Empowerment and Social Development on the Caribbean.** Kingston, Jamaica: Canoe Press.

Glazer, N., Creedon, C. (1970). **Children and Poverty: Some Sociological and Psychological Perspectives.** Chicago: Rand McNally.

Goodenough, Harris. (1998). **The Goodenough-Harris Draw A Man Test Manual,** Gale Encyclopedia of Childhood and Adolescence. Gale Research.

Hamilton, G.V. (1923). _Eysenck's Theories of Anxiety and Hystoria – A Methodological Critique._ **British Journal of Psychology,** Vol. 50, p.48-93.

Harriot, A. (2003). **Understanding Crime in Jamaica: New Challenges for Public Policy.** Kingston, Jamaica: UWI Press.

Henggeler, S.W. (1989). _Delinquency in Adolescence._ California: Sage.

Herbert, M., & Harper-Douton, K.V. (2000). **Working with Children, Adolescents and Their families.** Third Edition. Chicago, Illinois: Lyceum Books Inc.

Hoghughi, M. (1985). _Residential Care and Education._ Unpublished lecture. University of Newcastle Upon Tyne, England.

Hess, P., Howard, T. (1981). _An Ecological Model for Assessing Psychological Difficulties in Children._ Child Welfare Vol. LX, No. 8. New York: Child Welfare League of America.

Huizinga, Elliot, D., Esbenen, F. (1998). _The Denver Youth Survey Projects, Report No. 2._ University of Colorado, Boulder, USA.

Jayaratne, S., Stuart, R., & Tripodi, T. (1974). _Methodological Issues and Problems in Evaluating Treatment Outcomes in the Family and School Consultation Project._ In P. Davidson, F. Clark, & L. Hamerlynck (Eds.), Evaluation of behavioral programs in community, residential, and school settings. Champaign, IL: Research Press.

Jones, E. (1986). _"The social status of the Jamaican child"._ Paper presented at the First Children's Lobby Conference of Child Advocates, Caenwood Centre, Ministry of Education, Youth and Culture.

Jongsma, A.E., Peterson, L.M., & McInnis, W.P. (2003). **The Adolescent Psychotherapy Treatment Planner.** (Third Edition). Hoboken, New Jersey, John Wiley & Sons.

Kadushin, A. (1967). Child Welfare Services. New York: MacMillan.

Kelly, L. (1995). **Surviving Sexual Violence.** London: Polity Press.

Kernberg, P. & Chazen, F. (1991). **Children with Conduct Disorders.** Basic Books. New York.

Kleg, G. and Bandura A. (1973). *A Social Learning Analysis*. In Bandura, A., & Walters, R.H.I *Aggression*. Englewood Cliffs, New Jersey: Prentice-Hall.

Khron, M.D., Massey, J. (1980). Social Control and Delinquent Behaviour: An Examination of the Elements of Social Bonding. *The Sociological Quarterly*, Autumn: 529-543.

Lesser, J., Cooper, M., (2005). *Clinical Social Work Practice: An Integrated Approach*. Pearson, Allyn & Bacon, New York.

Levy, H., (1996). *They Cry 'Respect': Urban Violence and Poverty in Jamaica*. UWI Mona: Centre for Population, Community and Social Change.

Lewis, D.O. (1985). *Conduct Disorder and Juvenile Delinquency*. In H.I. Kaplan & B.J. Sadack (Eds.), *Comprehensive textbook of psychiatry*. Baltimore: Williams & Wilkins.

Lewis, D.O., Balla, D.A., Shanok, S.S., & Snoll, L. (1976). *Delinquency, Parental Psychopathology and Parental Criminality*. Journal of the American Academy of Child Psychiatry, 15(4), 665-678.

Marsh, O.D. (1994). *Children in Especially Difficult Circumstances, Policy Development and Review of Legislation in Jamaica*. Kingston, Jamaica: Child Support Unit, Ministry of Youth and Local Government, UNICEF.

Mass, H.S., Engler, E. (1959). *Children in Need of Parents*. New York: Columbia University Press.

McMahon, R.J. & Wells, K.C. (1991). Conduct Disorders. In Mash, E.J., & Barkley, R.L., (eds.) *Treatment of Conduct Disorders*. New York: Guilford.

Milbourne, P. (1989). *Child Abuse in Jamaica*. Child Guidance Clinic, Kingston, Jamaica: Unpublished Report commissioned by UNICEF.

Morrison, L. (1995). *Teach me a Better Way to Live*. Kingston, Jamaica: G&M Associates.

Orcutt, J.D. (1987). *Analyzing Deviants*. Homewood, Illinois: Dorsey Press.

Patterson, G.R., Debarshe, R., Barbara, D., Ramsay, E., (1989). *A Developmental Perspective on Anti-Social Behaviour. The American Psychologist*. American Psychological Association. February.

Patterson, V., Wood, K. (1993). Unpublished study of child care institutions in Kingston and St. Andrew. Kingston, Jamaica: Department of Sociology and Social Work, University of the West Indies.

Phillips, A. (1973). *Adolescence in Jamaica*. Kingston, Jamaica: Kingston Publishers.

Planning Institute of Jamaica (PIOJ). (1992). *Situation Analysis of Women and Children in Jamaica*. Kingston, Jamaica: PIOJ.

_____. (1995a). *Survey of Living Conditions*. Kingston, Jamaica: PIOJ.

_____. (1995b). *The National Plan of Action: Goals for Jamaican Children to the Year 2000*. Kingston, Jamaica: UNICEF.

_____. (1995c). *Situation Analysis of Women and Children in Jamaica*. Kingston, Jamaica: UNICEF.

_____. (2001). *The Jamaican Child*. Kingston, Jamaica.

Reiner, B., Kaufman, I. (1963). *Character Disorders in Parents of Deliquents*. New York: Family Services Association of America.

Richman, L.C., & Harper, D.C. (1979). *Parental child-rearing characteristics and delinquent adoles-cents' response to behavioral treatment*. American Journal of Orthopsychiatry, 49, 527-529.

Ritter, B. (1988). *Sometimes God Has a Kid's Face: The Story of America's Exploited Street Children*. New York: Covenant House.

Rosse, A.S., Kegan, J., Hareven, T., eds. (1978). *The Family*. New York: W.W. Norton.

Rutter (1972)...

Rutter, M., & Giller, H. (1983). *Juvenile Delinquency Trends and Perspectives*. New York: Penguin.

Sabatini, F., Newman-Williams, S. (1997). *Child Poverty in the Caribbean*. In Girvan, N., ed. *Poverty, Empowerment and Social Development in the Caribbean*. Kingston, Jamaica: Canoe Press.

Samms-Vaughan, M. (2001). *Cognition, Educational Attainment and Behaviour in a Cohort of Jamaican Children*. Policy Development Unit, Working Paper No. 5.

Samms-Vaughan, M., Jackson, M., Ashley, D., Lambert, M. (2005). *Jamaican Children's Experience of Corporal Punishment at Home and at School*. In Payne, M. (1989). *Use and Abuse of Corporal Punishment: A Caribbean View of Child Abuse & Neglect*. 13.

Sayle, E. (1994). *The First Fifty Years*. Kingston, Jamaica: Kingston Publishers.

Schior, D., (1983). Socialization: The Political Aspects of Delinquency Explanation. *Sociological Spectrum*, (Jan.-Mar.): pp.85-100.

Semaj, L., Redfearn, C. (1986). An Evaluation of Children's Homes in Jamaica. Unpublished study. Kingston, Jamaica: Caribbean Child Development Centre.

Shaw, C.R., McKay, H.D., (1931). *Are Broken Homes a Causative Factor in Juvenile Delinquency?* Social Forces, 1932, 10, pp.514-524.

Shaw, C.R., McKay, H.D., McDonald, J. (1938). *Brothers in Crime*. University of Chicago. Chicago, Illinois.

Smith, T.E. (1981). *Migration in the Commonwealth Caribbean: Flows and policies*. London: MacMillan.

Stuart, R., Jayaratne, S., Tripodi, T., Camburn, D, (1976). *A Experiment in Social Engagement in Serving the Families of Pre-Delinquents. Journal of Abnormal Psychology*, Volume 4, pp.170-188.

The Keating Report, Child Development Agency, Ministry of Health, Kingston, Jamaica.

Thomas-Hope, E. (1992). *Explanation in Caribbean Migration*. Warwick University Caribbean Studies. London: MacMillan Press.

Tomlinson, K. (2010 June). Resistance factors of children in state run institutions. Master's Thesis. UWI Mona: Department of Psychology, Sociology and Social Work.

Tomlinson, R., Petos, P. (1981). *"Alternatives to placing children: therapy with disengaging families"*, Child Welfare: *Journal of Policy, Practice and Programme* 60, No. 2.

United Nations Children's Fund (UNICEF). (1986). *Children at Risk in Jamaica Data Sheet*. Kingston, Jamaica: UNICEF.

UNICEF Report (2006). *Violence and Children in Jamaica*. Kingston, Jamaica.

_____. (2007). *Situation Analysis of Women and Children*. (Update). Gender Disparities in Jamaica.

Ward, E., Mansingh, A., Ramphal, P. (2001). *The Nature of Interpersonal Violence in Jamaica and its Strain on the National Health Services*, *West Indian Medical Journal*, 42: 53-56.

Warsh, R., Maluccio, A., Pine, B. (1994). *Teaching Family Reunification: A Source Book*. Washington, DC.: The Child Welfare League.

Wilson, L., Green, J. (1983). *"An experiential approach to cultural awareness in child welfare"*, Child Welfare: *Journal of Policy, Practice and Programme* 62, No. 4.

Abbreviations

ACT NOW – Assessment Counseling and Training Materials for Caribbean Populations

CARICOM – Caribbean Community

CDA – Child Development Agency

CXC – Caribbean Examinations Council

CSME – Caribbean Single Market Economy

DNA – Di-Nucleic Acid

GDP – Gross Domestic Product

JIS – Jamaica Information Service

JCC – Jamaica Council of Churches

CDA – Child Development Agency

CDC – Caribbean Child Development Centre

CPTC – Creative Production and Training Centre

GDP – Gross Domestic Product

GSAT – Grade Nine Achievement Test

KMR – Kingston Metropolitan Region

MOE – Ministry of Education

MOH – Ministry of Health

OCA – Office of the Children's Advocate

PTSD – Post Traumatic Stress Disorder

TAICC – Trauma Assessment Instrument for the Caribbean Child

UNICEF – United Nations Children's Education Fund

UWI – University of the West Indies

UWIVPP – University of the West Indies Violence Prevention Programme

VPA – Violence Prevention Alliance

APPENDIX I

Table Showing Comparative GDP among Caribbean Island

Country	Size (km2)	HDI Rank	GDP per capita (US$)	GDP growth rate 2004 (est.)	GDP per capita annual growth rate	Total debt-service (as %of GDP) 1990-2001
Antigua and Barbuda	442	56	9,961	1.0	2.7	114
Belize	22,960	67	3,258	3.0	1.6	93
Grenada	345	93	3,965	4.5	2.9	112
Guyana	214,970	92	912	2.4	4.4	200
Jamaica	11,424	78	3,005	2.1	(0.5)	139.4
St. Kitts and Nevis	269	51	7,609	2.4	3.9	160

(Sources: UNDP, 2003; Caribbean Development Bank, 2003; IMF, 2003; Planning Institute of Jamaica).

APPENDIX II

Incidence of children killed in Jamaica (by cause)

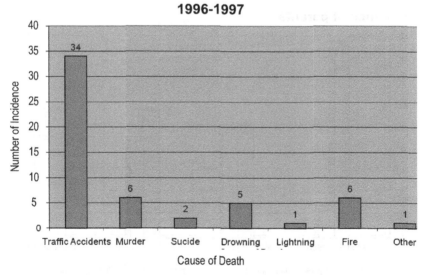

Incidence of children killed in Jamaica (by cause)
1998-2001

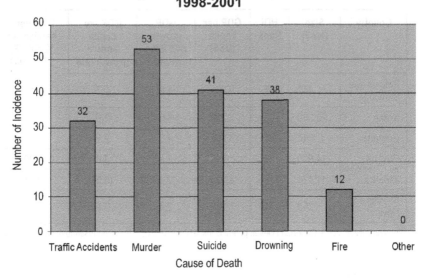

APPENDIX III

Absence of parents

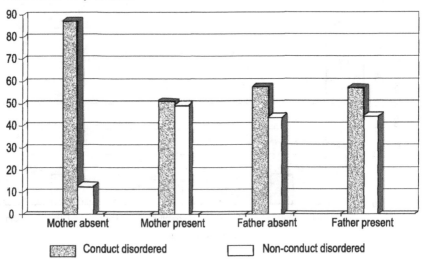

APPENDIX IV

Oval chart: Factors causing violence at the different levels of society

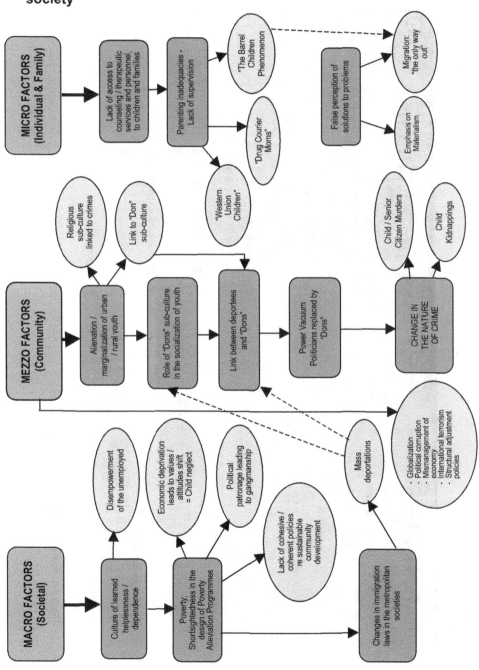

APPENDIX V

TAICC – Trauma Instrument for Caribbean Children

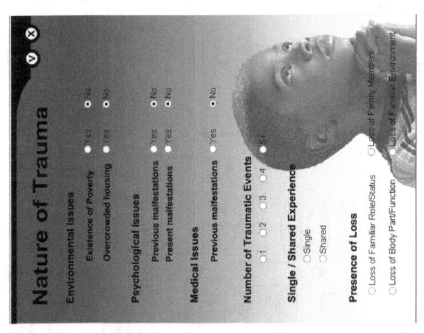

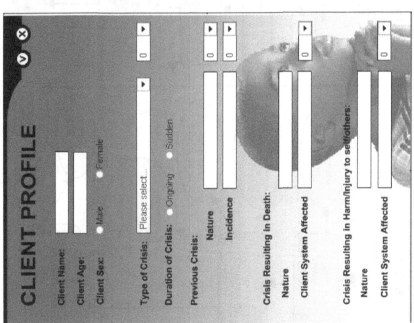

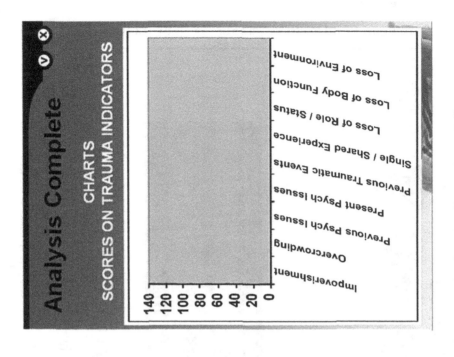

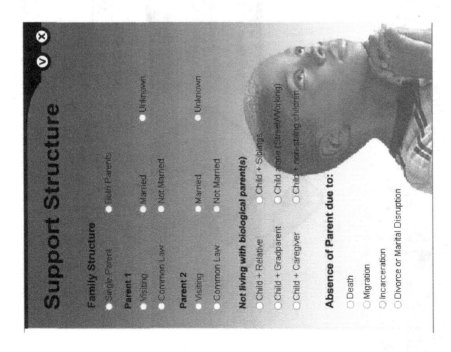

APPENDIX VI

Caribbean Child Welfare Resources Network (CCWRN)

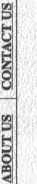

Caribbean Child Welfare
RESOURCE NETWORK
FOR CHILDREN & FAMILIES

ABOUT US
PHOTOS
CONTACT

Home

RESOURCES
STATISTICS
FORUM
INFO. CTR.
LIBRARY

Home

AGENCY RESOURCES

STATISTICS

CHILD WELFARE FORUM

INFORMATION CENTRE

PUBLICATIONS and LIBRARY

ABOUT US | CONTACT US

http://www.jcwrn.org

Product of ACT NOW Ltd.   (copyright 2007)

Developed by: Claudette Crawford Brown PhD., Lecturer, Department of Sociology, Psychology and Social Work,
University of the West Indies (Mona), Kingston, Jamaica

APPENDIX VII

ACT NOW social intervention tools

ACT NOW

What is ACT NOW

ACT NOW is a limited liability company that is committed to the development and production of culturally appropriate training materials and counselling tools for Caribbean populations.

Who Does It Serve?

ACT NOW provides products and services to parents and professionals, including social workers, guidance counsellors, state social service agencies, educational institutions, summer camps, and other organizations working with children at risk and children in difficult circumstances.

ACT NOW provides the following products:
- Puppet Theatre and Puppet Sets
- Workbooks
- Therapeutic Games & Manuals
- Training Manuals
- Story Books
- Posters
- Parenting Took Kit and Resource Materials
- Videos, CD ROMS and DVDs
  (Migration, Childhood Depressions & Suicide, Incest, Child Abuse, Violence)

ACT NOW provides the following services:
- Online Parent Support Systems
- Assessment Systems for Professionals
- Lending Library
- Training Workshops & Consultation Services: schools, summer camps, organizations, and social service agencies.
- Direct counselling services for individuals and families.

ACT NOW

Violent Prevention, Anger Management and Crisis Management Programmes for Primary and High Schools

ACT NOW has developed a multi-modal model of training products for Caribbean children in the general school population, as well as children with specialized emotional and behavioural needs. These methods are rooted in research and the experiences of scores of Caribbean professionals. They include:

1. After school & community programmes for At Risk youth—"The Conflict Zone' ©2000.
2. School-wide Behaviour clinic Programme—"The Behaviour Hype Zone" ©2003.
3. Peace Promotion, Peer Mediation & Intervention Programmes — "The Peace Warriors" ©2003. "The Peace Place" ©2003.
4. Summer Camp Consultations—Training of Camp Counsellors.
5. Provision of counseling aids, products and tools for counsellors and other professionals.
6. Training for Teachers & Guidance Counsellors—Crisis Management for dealing with Violence, Sudden Loss in Schools/Safe School Programmes.
7. Advanced Training for Social Service Professionals - Grief Bereavement and Loss, Play Therapy, Behaviour Modification, Sexual Abuse Counselling, Violence and Trauma Intervention. (Restrictions Apply)
8. Training for Community Police—Domestic Abuse, Sexual Abuse Referral.

The following series of Counseling Aids & Tools are now available for Caribbean Professionals.

APPENDIX VIII

Trends in overal crime rate 1996-2004

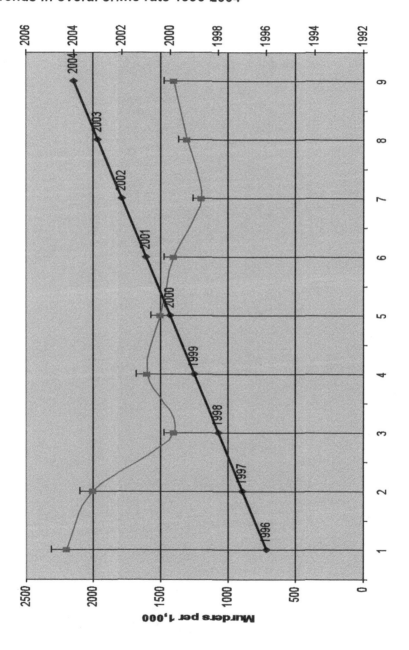

APPENDIX IX

APPENDIX IX

A Blue Print for Action – Managing violence in the home, school and country

The following section, "A Blue Print for Action", represents a user-friendly matrix of solutions for managing violence in homes, schools and communities.

Introduction to "A Blue Print for Action"

The solutions presented earlier in this chapter as recommendations are on target for the most part and form the basis for the proposals made in this "Blue Print." There is a dearth of information in the literature on the specific action-based strategies that need to be adopted in order to fulfill these recommendations. These proposals are set out as prescriptions for action by professionals, parents and other practitioners, who may need some direction as to how to intervene when specific problems confront them in their homes, schools, or communities. This user-friendly information is presented in chart form and is designed for use by school and community-based professionals with PTAs and other community groups.

Managing Violence in the Community

Presenting Problems	Intervention Strategy	Rationale for Intervention	Resources	Measurement Indicators
1. Overt exposure of children to community violence	• Development of safe play spaces & "Healing Gardens" for children at risk for violence • Use of art, interactive sculpture, puppetry to encourage children to express their feelings of loss /trauma	• To make children "precious" again at the community and societal level	- Ministry of Agriculture - School-based gardeners	• No. of after school programmes developed at the community level (primary all age and secondary in particular)
	• Use of pocket parks for transmitting oral history through elders to children using drama, music, etc. (e.g. Nanny's drama club model at Admiral Town) • Use of simple outdoor play spaces and gardens for use as reflection areas	• To encourage interaction between the elderly, adolescents & children, and so reduce instances of teen pregnancy and help the youth regain respect for the elderly, and childhood	- NHT - Ministry of Housing	• No. of play spaces/parks developed for purpose designated per community/ parish

Managing Violence in the Community

Presenting Problems	Intervention Strategy	Rationale for Intervention	Resources	Measurement Indicators
	• Use of police stations and school facilities for after school & weekend programmes for children at risk for violence • Establish open spaces for community performances	• To provide supervised spaces where socio-educational play and academic work (homework) can be completed in a safe environment • To provide opportunity for assessment and interaction with targeted youth at risk for violence, as victims and as perpetrators	- Ministry of Education (Guidance & Counselling) - NGOs	• No. of successful after school programs developed at the community level. (primary all-age, and secondary schools in particular)
	• Comprehensive Parenting Education programmes where children and parents attend as family groups		- SDC - Min. of National Security (Community aides)	• Successful implementation of Mentorship Programme
	• Mentorship programmes using police and/or adolescent mentors as role models			
	• Provide group parenting support in weekly community sessions for parents only- (fathers and mothers, fathers only, and mothers only) • Parenting Education Using "The Comfort Zone" model, grief counseling for children and families in 'war-torn' communities	• To assist parents in ventilating their issues in an environment where they can receive support from professionals and other parents • To target criminalized families and criminalized/garrison communities	- Parenting organizations - Peace management organizations	• No. of meetings held and attendance rates of parents
	• Provide programme where parents can receive advice and counseling on child rearing in a violent society • Using Healing Gardens, Healing Trees & other ameliorative activities	• To ensure that parents and children who are victims of violence receive effective and accessible counselling services	- NGOs providing grief and bereavement counselling.	• No. of Agencies providing accessible counselling programmes for individuals and families
2. Influence of self-imposed "community leaders" on the socialization of children	• Parenting education on problems & consequences of dependence on "loan sharks" and child predators • Providing alternatives for child support through well-developed measured social support programme for families	• To reduce the influence of negative adult role models in the socialization of children at the community level	- Social Development Commission (SDC) - Community churches - Youth development agencies - Police youth clubs - Child Development Agency - Correctional services	• Increase in no. of families using social welfare benefits from state agencies

Managing Violence in the Community

Presenting Problems	Intervention Strategy	Rationale for Intervention	Resources	Measurement Indicators
		• To reduce sexual exploitation of children by providing direct economic and material support to their families, eg., Basic food and school tuition and book assistance	- Provide education in schools on child safety & child protection from sexual predators (parents and children) - PATH/PASS programme	• Provide after-school community-based homework events & activity programmes where children can be engaged & evaluated
	• Government to regain its position as main provider of social welfare	• To reduce number of children exposed to sexual exploitation and violence due to economic needs & hardships	- Develop 1ft. law of mechanism to build abduction & predator accountability	
3. Influence of child sexual predators at community level	• Educate and expose girls and boys through infusion of self-esteem; development in curriculum of all-age & high schools • Help children to understand the importance of their own independence	• To reduce number of latency-aged girls & adolescents who depend on males for their survival	- Enforced parenting education sentences for adult parents whose children receive Fit Person Orders and Correctional Orders within the court system - Influence of parenting, self-esteem....Intelligence in girls & boys at pre & junior high schools	• Presentation of child predators sexual abuses
4. Societal breakdown in the ethics of parenting	• Massive public education programmes through large community based all-island fair on parenting	• To sensitize public to the need for benefits of parenting	- Corporate sponsors - Jamaica Information Service - Ministry of Health - Use of popular music/celebrities	• No. of parents who attend community force
5. Childhood under threat	• Demarcation of the boundaries of childhood through: - public education - advocacy - community based parenting curriculum - training of targeted Community practitioners - use of existing church programmes - strengthening existing best practice NGO programmes	• To make childhood "precious again" • To provide nurturing environment where children can grow to their maximum potential	-JIS -CPTC -JCC	• No. of parents who receive parenting information and attend parenting sessions • Changes in parenting practices • No. of trainings completed • Positive evaluation of training

Managing Violence in the Community

Presenting Problems	Intervention Strategy	Rationale for Intervention	Resources	Measurement Indicators

	• Use community-based parenting training educational programmes in schools/community centres
	  - use DVDs, brochures, billboards, posters
	  - Parenting training
	• Mandate media to introduce child-friendly, intelligent children's programming.
	• Massive media campaign using slogans such as "Make childhood precious again"
	• Educate the public regarding child safety policies to set appropriate boundaries for children's music, dress, and conduct, such as concerts, musical events...
		• To involve community members at all levels and train them as "violence interrupters," and "violence diversion agents"
		• To encourage a new generation of emotionally intelligent children
			- SDC
			- Peace Management Initiative
			- Min. of National Security
			- NGOs
				• No. of media programmes established to fulfill mandate

Managing Violence in Schools

Presenting Problems	Intervention Strategy/ Activities	Rationale for Intervention	Resources	Measurement Indicators

1.
• Damage to school property
• Littering/Graffiti
• Disregard for out of bounds ruling
	• Schools as safety zones
	• Monitoring & enforcement
	• Develop school pride:
	  - Classroom decorating competition
	  - Classroom door decorating competition
	  - House gardens
	  - Adopt a flower bed
		• To create in students a sense of pride in the appearance of their school	- School safety officers
			- Security guards & other security staff
			- Prefects
			- Alumni
				• Improvement in aesthetic appearance of school

2. Lack of solidarity in their school as an institution:
  - poor grooming
  - lack of adherence to dress code/uniform details (pins/ties/ epaulettes/belts, etc.)
	• Monitoring and Enforcement	• To create a sense of price and identity in one's school vs. other schools	- School safety officers	• Improved sense of pride in school
				• Reduced number of demerits for lack of uniform, etc.

Managing Violence in Schools

Presenting Problems	Intervention Strategy/ Activities	Rationale for Intervention	Resources	Measurement Indicators
3. Weakening of student leadership (e.g., student councils & leadership groups such as other students as peer counsellors) - Peer Mentorship ops - Peer Mediation ops	• Incentives for student participation • House points • Awards/prizes for student participation	• To make it desirable to be a student leader • Make it desirable to be good role models	- School as Safety Zone officers Package - Behaviour Hype Zone Package - High Profile Peer Mediation Programmes requiring training - Link to employment/ jobs	• Increased participation of students in leadership programmes
4. Physical loop holes in school security systems - Absence of perimeter fencing - Lack of security systems - Need for additional security for search and seizure - border security (gates).	• Enforcement of borders	• To create secure physical borders	- PTA Strategic Plan - School safety officers	• Reduced number of break-ins; authorized persons on school compound

Managing Violence in the Home

Presenting Problems	Intervention Strategy / Activities	Rationale for Intervention	Resources	Measurement Indicators
1. Reducing Incidence/ Prevention of Child Abuse and Neglect in the Home	• Improve Training of Social workers & other professionals in the assessment, intervention, & care management of child abuse and neglect in the home	• To ensure standards for assessment & treatment of Child Abuse are established as part of set protocol of operations. This should include standards that are mandated within the school system as well as at the community level	- SDC (community para-professionals) - Ministry of Education (Guidance & Counselling Unit) - Social Workers for the school system - Certified Training Organisation	• Number of professionals completing mandatory reporting training in different sectors - Medicine - Social Work - Education

Managing Violence in the Home

Presenting Problems	Intervention Strategy / Activities	Rationale for Intervention	Resources	Measurement Indicators
	• Enforce mandatory reporting of child abuse and neglect through specialized sensitization of professionals regarding mandatory reporting via DVD/video	• Link to professional licensing would ensure that professionals have input in the changing of operators and treatment professionals	- Network of CDA officers - Dept. of Correctional Officers - Health professionals - Teaching professionals (see above)	• Increased numbers of professionals reporting cases of child abuse and neglect
	• Incorporate mandatory reporting into core performance indicators for discerning requirements for professionals, e.g. social workers, doctors, and guidance counselors	• To improve levels of service delivery offered by professionals in the Child Welfare system and Health Service system, to victims and perpetrators of child abuse and neglect	- Primary Health Care professionals - Social Work professionals - Teaching professionals - All social service professional Associations responsible for licensing	• Improved licensing and certification systems for all professionals working with victims and perpetrators of Child Abuse and Neglect
2. Managing Unresolved Grief and Bereavement Issues	**Access to Service** • Improve all island access for children and families needing grief counseling and ameliorative/ supportive counseling through NGOs and state agencies, e.g. CDA	• To ensure that all children and families experiencing unresolved grief reactions, and those needing bereavement counseling have access to supportive counseling services as soon as/as long as needed	- UWI Violence Prevention Clinic Model - Other Best Practice Models - CDA - Ministry of Health/Education	• Improved management of cases of unresolved grief & loss • Improved reporting and referral of cases to counseling and other agencies
3. Managing Unresolved Grief and Bereavement	• Provide Social Agencies with Public Education material to help parents understand the need for grief and bereavement counselling	• To make grief and bereavement counselling widely available to the general populace • To ensure that families and professionals understand that unresolved grief is an issue that may need professional attention	- Jamaica Council of Churches - All professional Social Work Agencies - CDA - Dept of Corrections - NGOs	• Increased number of Social Service Agencies providing grief and bereavement counselling services

Managing Violence in the Home

Presenting Problems	Intervention Strategy / Activities	Rationale for Intervention	Resources	Measurement Indicators
	Healing Gardens/Adventure therapy • Provide outdoor spaces for children & families where healing can take place. - using flowers, sculpture,& interactive play areas in the community, through churches and other community centers - Programme could be integrated with "creating safe play spaces for children - Pocket Park programme which each government housing area/scheme has designated play area using flowers, sculpture etc. for play/relaxation. This would ensure de-stressing zones for families constantly in the line of fire	• To use the resource of good weather & natural beauty which abounds in the Caribbean as a readily available counselling aid	- Edna Manley School Of Art and UTECH Caribbean School of Architecture students - NHT PIOJ, Ministry of Housing /Ministry of Education	• Increased number of parks designated for children as well as an increase in the sections of public parks designated for children's play
	• Training of Guidance counselors & teachers to assess and detect unresolved grief	• To ensure standardization of assessment and treatment protocols in the school system	- Min. of Education (Guidance and Counselling Unit)	• Decreased numbers of cases of unresolved grief being referred to Psychiatric Departments
4. Managing Trauma Reactions - Depression - Apathy ("Ah Nuh Nutten" syndrome) - Post Traumatic Stress Disorder	• Develop and strengthen access to specialized counseling services for children of families experiencing trauma reactions. This will require all island availability for: - Assessment Services - Intervention Services - Case Management Follow-up Services	• To broaden the scope of existing counseling agencies by providing specialized assessment of intervention service for children & families traumatized by violence	- Ministry of Health-Mental Health system - Ministry of Education's Guidance Counsellors - Child Development Agency (CDA) - Other state social agencies	• Increased numbers of children being referred from schools or by their parents for counseling
	• Training of social workers, guidance counselors, & other mental health professionals in the Detecting, Assessment, Intervention and Case Management techniques to deal with childhood trauma - Improve cadre of clinical psychologists to provide support to above professionals	• To improve the skill set of all professionals working with traumatized children to enable them to refer children appropriately.	- UHWI Child Health Clinic - Child Guidance Clinic - UWI Violence Clinic - Other specialized agencies providing services to children and families affected by trauma	• Decreased numbers of children referred for psychological problems resulting as complications of untreated Post-Traumatic Stress Disorder

Managing Violence in the Home

Presenting Problems	Intervention Strategy / Activities	Rationale for Intervention	Resources	Measurement Indicators
	• Use of early warning/detection systems in schools & social agencies to enable school professionals to recognize basic symptoms of PTSD and other trauma reactions	**Prevention of further Pathology** • To ensure that trauma reactions are resolved & processed by victims before they become internalized & lead to pathology	- "ACT NOW" "When You Need a Hug" counseling package - Other counseling tools: Trauma Intervention	• Reduction in numbers of children exhibiting symptoms of Post-Traumatic Disorder • Increased number of professionals able to assess and detect the range of symptoms being presented in Jamaica as trauma reactions

Managing Violence – Teacher-Centered Issues

Presenting Problems	Intervention Strategy &/ Activities	Rationale for Intervention	Resources	Measurement Indicators
1. Teacher-Teacher Violence	• Professional Development Sensitization on Conflict Resolution • Improve teacher morale • Team-building activities • Wellness programmes • Stress Busting Techniques	• To create zero tolerance for teacher-teacher violence	- JTA/Ministry of Education - School-based monitoring - Code of Conduct for Teachers/Professional Ethics Document - Guidance Counselling/School Social Values - JTA Disciplinary Policy	• Reduced/No incidence of teacher-teacher violence
2. Teacher-Student Altercations/Fighting	• Boundary setting • Stress busting techniques for teachers • Lunch hour rap sessions • Weekly teacher-teacher rap sessions • JTA monitoring & follow up	• To create zero tolerance for teacher-student violence	- Character/values programmes - School-based monitoring - JTA/Education officer - Guidance Counselling Unit/Social Work Division - Anger Management Programmes for Teachers	• Reduced incidence/No incidence of teacher-student altercations

Managing Violence – Teacher-Centered Issues

Presenting Problems	Intervention Strategy ß/ Activities	Rationale for Intervention	Resources	Measurement Indicators
3. Student-Teacher Altercations: physical/ verbal - Assault - Involvement of parents/ community/relatives	• Boundary setting • Standardize policy re corporal punishment (e.g., age limit vs. total elimination)	• To create zero tolerance in student-teacher assault	- School safety officers (retired police) - Character/Values Programme - schools as safety zones	• Reduced incidence of student-teacher altercations - physical/ verbal
4. Teacher-Student Sexual Harassment/Abuse (link to student recommenda-tions /grades)	• Code of Conduct • Clear policies & reporting procedures for student complaints • Monitoring/reinforcement • Protection re. false claims - JTA	• Zero tolerance of teacher-student sexual harassment/ abuse	- 'School as safety zone' package - Principal - Supported by JTA policies	• Reduced incidence of teacher-student sexual behaviour
5. Student-Teacher Sexual Overtures	• Training of young teachers and new recruits • Boundary setting	• To help student understand-ing of teacher-student boundaries	- Principal/Staff - Senior Prefects	• Reduced incidents of student-teacher sexual overtures

APPENDIX X

SUMMER CAMP METHODOLOGY

INTERVENTION MODEL USED

The model chosen for the process of identifying children who needed specialized intervention was a model of Community Care using specially trained alternative Care Givers who were chosen on the basis of the extent to which they represented a range of individuals at the community level to whom the children could go to for help and assistance. This model is an experimental one being used currently at the UWI Violence Programme for working with children who are perpetrators of violence. This model was therefore tested within the context of the intervention, at a summer camp for violence prevention.

The counselling staff was therefore structured to provide services at two levels:

(A) Peer/Junior Counsellors who were highly educated and motivated community youngsters who were role models, and who lived in and around the communities where the children resided. (23 in number)

(B) Senior Counsellors Highly trained and experienced clinicians 5 of whom had worked with the core group of 35 children at the Shortwood Practising School. (12 in number) were used. This group was supplemented by a group of community paraprofessionals, handpicked to provide a core of community care, using a nurturant method of intervention, within the framework of the overall Community Care Model which included lots of hugs and gentle but firm discipline through structured intervention. Activity workbooks developed by the UWI Violence Prevention Programme were used. This group included a Rastafarian, a grandfather and a "grandmotherly" figure, as well as young university students who were volunteers (5 in number).

SHORTWOOD SCORES

Chart 1.

Names	Antisocial Behaviour	Anger Control	Emotional Distress	Positive Self
A	● ●		●	
B		●	●	
C		●		
D	●	●		
E	● ●		●	
F		●		●
G	● ●	●	●	
H			●	
I		●	●	
J	● ●		●	
K	● ●		●	●
L			●	
M				
N	●	●		
O			● ●	● ●
P		●	●	
Q		●	●	
R			● ●	●
S				
T	● ●		●	

● Blue represents the lower range of undesireable behaviour
● Red represents the upper range of undesireable behaviour

METHODOLOGY

Daily and intensive counselling was provided for two hundred (200) children one hundred and thirty boys (130), and seventy (70) girls, for a two week period. There were minor fluctuations in these numbers daily. The problems presented by the campers approximated those that had already been seen in the in-school mentoring programme. The emotional and behavioural problems identified by the counselling team after three months of working once per week with these children, within the school from March to June, included among other factors:

o Depression
o Unresolved Grief
o Emotional Neglect
o Physical Neglect
o Sexual Abuse, (Victims, and Perpetrators)
o Attention Deficit Hyperactivity Disorder, and
o Conduct Disorder (Childhood Presentation)

Chart 2 Showing Emotional & Behavioural Problems in Summer Campers

KEY (For all figures)   **SBP** (Severe Behavioural Problems) **MBP** (Moderate Behavioural Problems) **EP** (Emotional Problems)

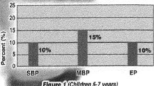

Figure 1 (Children 5-7 years)

SBP 10%   MBP 15%   EP 10%

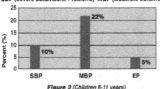

Figure 2 (Children 8-11 years)

SBP 10%   MBP 22%   EP 5%

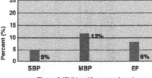

Figure 3 (Children 12 years and over)

SBP 5%   MBP 12%   EP 6%

FINDINGS

The counsellors interacted with the campers as a large group but in addition, campers who seemed to present with specific problems, were counselled on the basis of a daily referral system. In using this system, the junior counsellors regularly referred children to the team of senior counsellors who worked with them for three hours every afternoon in concert with the junior counsellors who assisted during this time with bathroom breaks and general maintenance of the children's basic needs.

The children who were referred fell into three large groups as follows:

A. Children with severe behavioural problems including Conduct Disorders (SBP)

B. Children with Symptoms of Inattentiveness and Hyperactivity only, including Attention Deficit Hyperactivity Disorder (MBP)

C. Children with Emotional Problems including Depression (EP)

AGE GROUP 5-7 YEARS
The children in this age group were the second most challenging group with 25% of the children having moderate to severe behavioural problems and 10% of them having emotional problems.

which seemed to be symptoms of childhood depression. (Please see (Chart 2 above)

AGE GROUP 8-11 YEARS
The children who presented with the most visible problems were children in the age group 8-11, where 32% had moderate to severe behavioural problems. (Please see Chart 2 above). The severe problems included fighting which occurred at least 2 to three times per day, whereas the moderate problems were mainly children with attention deficit hyperactivity disorder as set out by DSM IV and hyperactivity problems. The children with emotional problems which represented 5% of the group, mainly represented children who were depressed and who were victims of bullying and teasing.

AGE GROUP 12 AND OVER
The children in this group were the most "manageable" group and had the least problems in terms of the prevalence of behavioural problems (17%). These behavioural problems were mainly conduct disordered symptoms, which presented as fighting and verbal assault. The number of youngsters with emotional problems was (8%). These were again children who presented with symptoms of depression and exhibited symptoms of withdrawal from their peers. (Please see Chart 2 above).